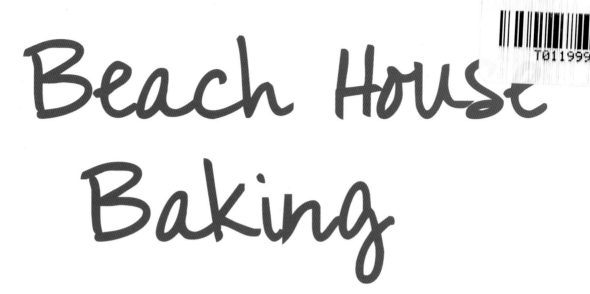

Beach House Baking

An Endless Summer of Delicious Desserts

Lei Shishak

Photographs by Chau Vuong

Skyhorse Publishing

Skyhorse Publishing books may be purchased in bulk at special discounts for sales promotion, corporate gifts, fund-raising, or educational purposes. Special editions can also be created to specifications. For details, contact the Special Sales Department, Skyhorse Publishing, 307 West 36th Street, 11th Floor, New York, NY 10018 or info@skyhorsepublishing.com.

Skyhorse and Skyhorse Publishing are registered trademarks of Skyhorse Publishing, Inc., a Delaware corporation.

www.skyhorsepublishing.com

10 9 8 7 6 5 4 3 2

Library of Congress Cataloging-in-Publication Data is available on file.

ISBN: 978-1-51071-925-5

Printed in China

*"It doesn't matter where you go in life . . .
as long as you go to the beach."*

contents

introduction

Journey to the beach. I wasn't always a beach girl. In fact, growing up in rural Pennsylvania I was more of a country bumpkin. And if that wasn't enough I spent four long cold winters in Maine during my college years before moving to Manhattan to begin a career in Private Banking. While the job did more than pay my bills, I was missing a creative outlet. I wanted to work with my hands and create. I wanted to work with food. I wanted to bake. But, I wondered, "Was I just being nostalgic recalling baking with my mom as a child? Was baking only meant to be a hobby for me? Did I really want to bake professionally?"

One morning on my way to the bank, I saw a small bakery with a "Now Hiring" sign hanging in the window. The bakery, Buttercup Bake Shop, was owned by Jennifer Appel, who co-founded the famed Magnolia Bakery. I somehow convinced her I was worth hiring and became a weekend cake decorator at her shop. Used to sitting at a cubicle all day, my body shut down after my first day on the job at the bakery. When I got back to my apartment, I soaked in epsom salt for hours and liberally applied Bengay onto my wrists and ankles until they were numb. I had never labored so hard—and I was only a part-time cake decorator! Thankfully, after my first week there, my body acclimated to the rigors of kitchen work, and I was on a perpetual high dreaming of a career in food. After over a year there, I left both my baking and banking jobs and enrolled at the Culinary Institute of America in upstate New York. It was there that I learned baking and pastry arts from some of the most knowledgeable chefs I have ever met. For all those who fear the demands and rigor of culinary school, yes, the Chefs will push you, but that's what you should want to be there for. After graduating at the top of my class with honors, it was time to head out West to the beach. California is not only a physical destination it's also a state of mind. I was eager, ready for a career change and felt like I was destined to do some great things. Quite frankly as well, I had spent the first 26 years of my life shoveling snow and scraping ice off of my windshield, and I was over it. I packed up my bags and headed to California.

I began working with Chef Scott Leibfried in Los Angeles. Though I was a lowly pastry cook, I was given great responsibility and was held to high standards. I learned to work efficiently and educated myself on the importance of using seasonal and fresh ingredients. After a stint at another popular Los Angeles restaurant I moved down the coast to Orange County and became the Executive Pastry Chef at Michael Mina's Stonehill Tavern at the St. Regis Monarch Beach. Moving to the fine dining realm was another unforgettable professional experience as I learned from some of the best front- and back-of-the-house experts. I learned the art of plating, the importance of paying attention to the details, and numerous innovative pastry techniques from Chef Lincoln Carson. I learned that the guest is always right (until you get off work and have a drink) and that it is far more fulfilling to create an unforgettable experience for a guest than to push your vision onto someone. After five incredible years at Stonehill Tavern it was time to go out on my own and start my own beach town bakery.

By now I had fallen in love with the beach lifestyle and knew that I could never leave. I chose to open my bakery in the beach town of San Clemente. Its low-key lifestyle and coastal location had always appealed to me and lucky for me, there was a dearth of bakeries in town. I opened Sugar Blossom Bake Shop in early 2010 and hit the ground running. To summarize, running your own business is both exhilarating and exhausting. Thankfully, with a lot of hard work has come much success. I could never have imagined how satisfying it would be to be an entrepreneur. Being the daughter of immigrants, I can attest to how lucky we are to live in America where opportunity is ours for the taking. It is refreshing to bake my own creations on a daily basis and see the smiles my sweet treats bring to people's faces. If there ever was a dream job for me, this is it.

Life at the beach. I can't imagine not living near the beach. Discovering secluded beaches and hidden coves, kayaking in the early mornings, watching the sun set, and exploring tidal pools are just some of the wonderful things I get to do every day because I live by the beach. I love the sound of waves crashing, the smell of ocean air, and the feel of the Pacific breeze through my hair. Everything seems better when done at the beach if you think about it: sipping a Bordeaux, sharing a secret, indulging in dark chocolate, setting up a picnic, receiving a proposal, sneaking in a workout, getting lost in a good read, firing up a barbeque, even taking a nap!

Baking by the beach. At home when I bake, the beach house fills with the most delicious aromas while the sunlight pours in through the tall windows above. I like to stand in these shafts of light to warm up while taking in a deep breath of the sweets I have baking in the oven. As I look out my loft windows, I see the infinity beyond the ocean and the view makes me feel like nothing is impossible, every day is another chance to do something good, and my life is such a gift.

I wanted to write this book so others could experience the beach lifestyle I and many others are fortunate to have. I get to bake every day in the prettiest place on earth. I wanted to share these tried and truly delicious recipes that I enjoy baking and sharing with everyone in my life. My high quality, made-from-scratch desserts will transport you to beaches and tropical paradises you've always hoped to visit. Not only will this book bring you into the kitchen, it will take you to places beyond.

tools

To make the best possible beach house treats, I've compiled a list of essential tools and equipment to have in your kitchen. If you don't have them all, don't fret—it's possible you may own a similar tool that will perform the same function just as well.

Oven

The recipes in this book were tested on a home gas range. Electric range ovens, as well as commercial convection ovens, can produce very different results. Make sure to adjust baking times accordingly. Also, since internal oven temperature often varies from the dial temperature, make sure to calibrate your oven with an *oven thermometer*.

Heavy-Duty Electric Mixer

This piece of equipment is worth the investment. The recipes in this book were tested on a 5-quart KitchenAid. Unless you're making larger batches, this size mixer will work just fine. If you're going to do a lot of baking, I highly recommend the commercial version, as it will last a long time and has the power to handle dense doughs. Your KitchenAid will come with a wire whisk, a dough hook, and one or two paddles.

Microwave Oven

Don't underestimate the essentialness of a microwave oven. I use it multiple times a day when baking at Sugar Blossom as well as at home. I use my microwave oven primarily for melting chocolate, warming up liquids, and softening butter and doughs when necessary.

Food Processor

For me, a food processor is a nice-to-have rather than a need-to-have. I've found that a *knife* and *cutting board* work just fine for chopping nuts. Both a *mortar and pestle* and a *coffee grinder* are great for pulverizing cookies for crusts.

Blender

I own an Oster 6-cup model, but any established blender brand will work well for making my frozen pop and beverage recipes. I also own a Hamilton Beach hand blender that works well for puréeing the pumpkin for my Candied Pumpkin Pie.

Juicer

I have a Waring Commercial model, but any established juicer brand will work well for making my frozen pop and beverage recipes. A hand-held metal juicer works great as well.

Electric Scale

Most of the ingredients in this book are measured in volume, some are given in weight. I highly recommend investing in a high-quality scale. Though I now own several, I still have my first one that I purchased years ago.

Waffle Press

You will need a waffle press to make my Buckwheat Wafflecakes. I own a Proctor Silex, but there are many suitable brands out there to choose from.

Baking Trays/Sheet Trays

You will find that I refer to baking trays and sheet trays interchangeably throughout this book. I am referring to what's also known as a *standard cookie sheet*. When I bake, I prefer to use a commercial half-sheet tray. It remains flat even after many uses at varying temperatures.

Stainless Steel Bowls

I own a number of stainless steel bowls of varying sizes. They are lightweight yet durable. You will find that they come in handy when scaling out ingredients and when hand mixing batters.

Cake Pans

You can bake any of the cupcake recipes in this book as a cake if you desire. I use sturdy aluminum cake pans with a 2-inch depth. Make sure to grease and line the pan bottoms with parchment paper circles before pouring in the batter. Cake pans come in various sizes and shapes, though the most popular are round 6-inch, 9-inch, and 12-inch pans. You can find them in commercial baking supply stores. Cheesecake is best baked in a *spring form pan*, which allows for a cleaner way of unmolding. For the recipes in this book, you will need a 9-inch round cake pan, 9-inch round spring form, 10-inch tube, 8-inch square, and 9x13-inch pan.

Pie Pans

I use 9-inch pie pans for the recipes in this book.

Cupcake Pans

Cupcake baking pans are available in three sizes: small (mini), medium (regular), and large (jumbo). This variety allows for experimentation with different cupcake forms. You can bake the cupcake recipes in this book in any size pan, although you'll need to adjust the baking times for mini and large pans. Mini cupcakes usually take 5 to 7 minutes less than regular-size cupcakes and jumbo cupcakes usually take 8 to 10 minutes more. I like to use the large cupcake pan for my Maple Pecan Sticky Buns.

Cooling Racks

For most of the recipes in this book, a cooling rack is a nice tool to have rather than something you need to have. In general, the textures of baked items are best when cooled on a wire rack. However, unless specified in the recipe, the treats in this book taste just as delicious when cooled in their pans.

Sieves/Sifters

I recommend purchasing a set of sieves of varying sizes. I use them regularly to sift dry ingredients before baking. I also use them when making the beverage recipes in this book.

Ice Cream Scoops

I prefer to use ice cream scoops to portion out my cupcake batters and cookie doughs. If you plan on doing a lot of baking, I recommend purchasing commercial scoops such as Vollrath. You can find them in many restaurant supply stores.

Measuring Cups and Spoons

One of the biggest mistakes home bakers make is using liquid measurement cups to scale out dry ingredients and vice versa. Make sure to purchase high-quality stainless cups and spoons as well as a Pyrex liquid measuring cup.

Offset Spatulas

I can never have too many offset spatulas, especially the mini ones, which are about 6-inches long. These are great for frosting cupcakes as well as smoothing out batters before baking.

Rubber Spatulas

Oh, how I love rubber spatulas! I recommend purchasing a few of these in varying sizes. Williams Sonoma and other specialty food stores carry high-quality spatulas.

Knives

I find that the two most useful knives when making the recipes in this book are a chef's knife and a paring knife. Make sure to purchase a *stone* and *steel* to keep your knives sharp.

Thermometer

There are two types of thermometers you should have: an oven and a hand-held. Over time, your oven's temperature may vary. It's a good idea to check your oven's temperature regularly to make sure it is calibrated properly. A hand-held battery operated thermometer is essential for making sure items are made and cooked to the right temperature.

Decorating Turntable

A turntable is a big expense, but well worth it, especially if you will be using my cupcake recipes to bake and decorate cakes. If you are serious about baking and creating the best-looking product possible, then splurge on a heavy-duty Ateco turntable with a cast-iron base and an aluminum top.

Parchment Paper/Aluminum Foil

You will use parchment paper and aluminum foil to line baking trays and cake pans. I prefer parchment paper, as it lays flat and doesn't tear as easily as aluminum foil.

Cupcake Liners

You can bake the cupcakes in this book in paper liners or in greased cupcake pans. I prefer paper liners most of the time because the cupcakes are easier to get out of the pan, easier to handle, and they stay fresh longer. These days, cupcake paper liners are available in a wide range of sizes, colors, and patterns.

Cardboard Rounds

If you plan to use my cupcake recipes to bake cakes, then you will need to purchase cardboard cake rounds. They come in various diameters, depending on the size of the cake you are making.

Disposable Pastry Bags

If you plan on doing a lot of decorating, it's worth buying disposable pastry bags. Even though they are disposable, you can wash and re-use them multiple times. It's also handy to have multiple bags when decorating with different tips and colors.

Decorating Tips

If you plan on doing a lot of decorating, I recommend purchasing a decorating tip set. They are inexpensive and will give you lots of decorating options.

Cookie Cutters

I recommend having a set of round and fluted cookie cutters. I prefer the Ateco brand.

Pastry Brush

Pastry brushes are used to spread butter, oil, or glazes on food or bakeware. They can be found at most department stores.

Torch

I suggest having a small butane torch for toasting meringue. You can purchase one at most restaurant supply stores.

Microplane

This is the best tool to extract zest from citrus.

ingredients

Butter
Use fresh, room temperature, unsalted butter unless otherwise specified.
1 cup = ½ pound = 8 ounces = 2 sticks

Eggs
Use room temperature Grade A large eggs unless the recipe calls for something different.

Extracts
Use pure rather than imitation-flavor extracts. It will make a big difference in the taste.

Liquids
Use room temperature liquids unless otherwise specified. If the liquids are stored in the refrigerator, warm them up in the microwave before using.

Milk
Use whole milk to get the best-tasting results.

Buttermilk
Use Grade A low-fat cultured buttermilk. In my experience, substitutions for buttermilk (e.g., whole milk and vinegar combined) are not conducive to the recipes in this book.

Flour
I recommend using cake flour for the cupcake and cake recipes. I recommend using all-purpose flour in the cookie recipes. Cake flour has a lower gluten protein content and, therefore, produces a lighter textured product than all-purpose flour.

Sugar
Granulated sugar is referred to as *sugar* in this book.

Brown Sugar
Always measure out packed brown sugar unless noted otherwise.

Powdered Sugar

Always sift powdered sugar before using.

Chocolate

I use a variety of chocolates in my recipes. Please make sure to use the specific type of chocolate I have listed in the recipe to ensure the best tasting beach house treat.

Cocoa Powder

For most of the recipes in this book, I prefer to use my favorite cocoa powder, Cacao Barry Plein Arôme. It is an unsweetened alkalized cocoa powder great for all-purpose baking and can be found at specialty food stores. Valrhona and Scharffenberger are other excellent brands.

Oats

I use old-fashioned 100 percent whole grain oats in my recipes. I refer to these as *rolled oats* in my recipes. Do not substitute with instant oatmeal.

Salt

Use table salt unless otherwise specified.

just a note about these recipes:

Recipes have been marked with the following
symbols when applicable:

♥   heart-healthy recipe

☼   perfect for picnics at the beach

v   vegan recipe

g   gluten-free recipe

⏰   quick-prep recipe

★   favorite recipe

morning treats

Many of us who live by the beach are early risers. To get our bodies and minds going so early in the day, morning nourishment is crucial. And, if you're like me, you're hungry the second you wake up.

While it would be lovely to have a complete breakfast every morning, most days I just don't have the time or desire to create a breakfast buffet. After all, less time inside means more time spent at the beach! So I've created some simple and delicious breakfast treats that are short on preparation and long on flavor. In fact, many of them can be made the day before so you can enjoy them as soon as you wake up.

All of the treats in this chapter are delicious on their own, but if you need something more to satiate your appetite, you can pair them with other breakfast items. For instance, my **Aged Cheddar, Bacon, and Scallion Biscuits** (page 15) are delectable with poached eggs and hollandaise sauce, while my **Daybreak Muffins** (page 12) pair perfectly with a cup of **Surfer Cowboy Coffee** (page 33). If you need something more nutritious yet substantial for breakfast, try mixing peanut butter into my **Beach's Best Granola** (page 11) and enjoy it with some apple slices.

I hope these sweet and savory treats will give you a great start to your day like they do mine. If you're not really a breakfast eater, pick one or two of these and try them. You may find it makes your mornings much brighter.

bountiful blueberry scones ★☼

Makes 6 Scones

2 cups all-purpose flour

⅓ cup sugar

1 teaspoon ground cinnamon

1 teaspoon baking powder

¼ teaspoon baking soda

¼ teaspoon salt

½ cup (1 stick) unsalted butter, cold

½ cup sour cream

1 large egg

2 tablespoons blueberry preserves

1 (4.4-ounce) package blueberries

2 teaspoons sugar for sprinkling

I prefer to enjoy these scones chilled.

The beautiful coastal state of Maine proudly boasts the wild blueberry as its state fruit. Located on Georgetown Island in Maine's mid-coast region near Bath, Reid State Beach is often called a beach bum's wonderland. This beach is a good place to spend some solitary time exploring tidal pools and climbing rocks at low tide. From Griffith Head, located inside the park, you can pause in awe of the majesty of Maine's shoreline, from its sandy beaches to its carved rock formations with the churning sea in the background. I spent my college years in this picturesque state, and every time I have a bite of these buttery, blueberry-filled scones, I am filled with images of all the hidden coastal beauty this state offers.

1 Preheat the oven to 400 degrees. Line a baking sheet with parchment paper or aluminum foil.

2 In a medium bowl, whisk together the flour, sugar, cinnamon, baking powder, baking soda, and salt. Grate the cold butter into the dry ingredients on the medium holes of a cheese grater. Quickly and gently work in the butter with your fingers before the butter gets soft. Set aside the mixture.

3 In a small bowl, whisk together the sour cream and egg until smooth. Pour over the flour and butter mixture. Use your hands to combine all the ingredients until the dough clumps together when gently squeezed. Place half the dough onto a clean, lightly floured surface. Pat into a 7-inch circle about ½-inch thick.

The dough will seem a bit dry and crumbly but will come together when patted down.

4 Spread the preserves over the top of the dough using a mini offset spatula. Add the blueberries on top of the preserves and sprinkle 1 teaspoon of sugar over the berries. Place the remaining dough over the blueberries and pat it down evenly over the fruit. Use one hand to cradle the edges while your other hand pats the dough down.

5 Sprinkle the dough with the remaining teaspoon of sugar and cut it into 6 triangles using a sharp knife. Place on the prepared baking sheet.

6 Bake for 20 to 22 minutes or until the tops of the scones bounce back when pressed gently. Let cool for at least 10 minutes before serving.

maple pecan sticky buns ★

Makes 6 buns

There's a beautiful view of the Pacific at the top of the street that runs by my bake shop in San Clemente. On Sunday mornings, as shoppers visit the open air farmers' market, they are surrounded by the delicious aroma of our freshly baked cinnamon rolls. This recipe is a twist on those cinnamon rolls. The buttermilk biscuit dough bakes in the maple pecan goo, creating a sticky sweet tender breakfast bun.

1 Preheat the oven to 400 degrees. Place a clean cookie tray on the middle rack. Generously butter then grease a 6-cup jumbo muffin pan with pan spray.

2 *Make the filling:* In a medium bowl, combine the sugars and cinnamon. Measure out the maple syrup and keep separate from the sugar-spice mixture.

3 *Make the topping:* In a 1-quart saucepan, combine the brown sugar, butter, maple syrup, and corn syrup over low heat. Stir until the sugar and butter are melted. Portion half of the hot syrup into each muffin cup as evenly as possible. Set aside the remaining syrup. Sprinkle the chopped pecans on top of the syrup. Set aside the prepared pan.

4 *Make the dough:* In an electric mixer fitted with a paddle attachment, mix the ricotta cheese, buttermilk, sugar, butter, maple syrup, and vanilla extract on low speed until combined. Small lumps of ricotta in the batter are fine. Add the flour, baking powder, salt, and baking soda. Mix until the dough comes together. The dough will be sticky.

On a floured work surface, roll out the dough into a rectangle 10 × 14-inches and ¼-inch thick. Roll the rectangle so a long side is facing you.

Using a pastry brush, paint the dough with the maple syrup. Sprinkle the sugar-spice mixture over the syrup as evenly as possible and pat it down.

Starting at the long edge nearest you, roll up the dough jelly-roll style. Pinch the seam to seal and leave the ends open. With a sharp knife or dental floss, cut the roll into 6 equal pieces, about 1½ inches wide. (At this point, the unbaked buns can be stored for later use. See the sidebar for instructions.) Place each bun into the prepared muffin pan.

5 Place the muffin pan in the oven on the cookie tray. Bake approximately 25 to 28 minutes or until they are golden brown and the centers are firm when gently pressed.

6 Remove pan from the oven. Immediately and carefully invert onto a serving tray. Let buns cool for 10 minutes, pour remaining syrup over the buns, and serve warm.

Filling
¼ cup light brown sugar, lightly packed
¼ cup sugar
1 teaspoon ground cinnamon
2 tablespoons Grade A medium amber maple syrup

Sticky Topping
1½ cups light brown sugar, lightly packed
1 cup (2 sticks) unsalted butter
6 tablespoons Grade A medium amber maple syrup
2 tablespoons light corn syrup
½ cup pecans, chopped

Dough
¾ cup ricotta cheese
¼ cup buttermilk
½ cup sugar
¼ cup (½ stick) unsalted butter, at room temperature
2 tablespoons Grade A medium amber maple syrup
1 teaspoon pure vanilla extract
2 cups all-purpose flour
1 tablespoon baking powder
½ teaspoon salt
¼ teaspoon baking soda

To get a head start on these buns, make the dough the day before. Wrap the unbaked sliced buns with plastic and store in refrigerator overnight. Take them out the next morning to come to room temperature while you make the sticky topping.

buckwheat wafflecakes ⏰♥

Makes about 15 wafflecakes

½ cup all-purpose flour

¼ cup buckwheat flour

¼ cup cornstarch

1 teaspoon sugar

½ teaspoon baking powder

¼ teaspoon baking soda

¼ teaspoon ground cinnamon

¼ teaspoon salt

1 large egg

½ cup buttermilk

½ cup whole milk

6 tablespoons canola oil

Grade A maple syrup for drizzling

As a child, I used to love eating toasted Eggo waffles and maple syrup. Now as a grown-up child, I still love the combination, but I've come up with a healthier take on the waffles so I don't feel as guilty when I eat them.

1 Preheat your waffle maker.

2 In a large bowl, whisk together the flours, cornstarch, sugar, baking powder, baking soda, cinnamon, and salt. Form a well in the center.

3 In a separate bowl, whisk together the egg, buttermilk, milk, and canola oil. Pour into the well and whisk just until ingredients are combined.

4 Drop a small amount (about ⅛ cup) of batter into the center of each waffle form. Close lid and cook for approximately 2 minutes. Flip waffles over with a fork, close lid and cook for 1 more minute. Remove from waffle maker, drizzle with maple syrup, and serve immediately.

lovers' coffee cake ★

Makes a 10-inch tube cake

Streusel

1 cup dark brown sugar
½ cup sliced almonds
¼ cup all-purpose flour
1 teaspoon ground cinnamon
¼ cup (½ stick) unsalted butter, melted

Cake

2 cups cake flour
1 teaspoon baking powder
1 teaspoon baking soda
½ cup (1 stick) unsalted butter, at room temperature
½ cup sugar
¼ cup dark brown sugar
2 large eggs
1 teaspoon pure vanilla extract
1 teaspoon pure almond extract
1 cup sour cream
1 pound sweet cherries, pitted

If fresh cherries aren't in season, I recommend substituting Trader Joe's Morello cherries. Simply drain and use.

Cherries are well-known to have aphrodisiac qualities. Not only is Oregon one of the primary producers of this stimulating fruit, it is also home to Neskowin Beach, one of the most romantic beaches on the Oregon Coast. Towering over this lovers' hideaway is Proposal Rock, a huge monolith jutting from the ocean. Legend claims that a local family had nine daughters, each of whom was proposed to near this giant rock. This is the perfect spot to enjoy this delicious cake, watch the sun rise, and hold on to the one you love.

1 Preheat the oven to 350 degrees. Liberally grease a 10-inch tube pan with pan spray.

2 *Make the streusel:* Combine the brown sugar, almonds, flour, cinnamon, and butter in a large bowl. Mix thoroughly and set aside.

3 *Make the cake:* Sift together the flour, baking powder, and baking soda. Set aside. In the bowl of an electric mixer fitted with the paddle attachment, cream the butter and sugars on medium speed for 2 minutes, until light and fluffy. With the mixer on low, add in the eggs and extracts and mix until combined. Scrape down the bowl. Add in half of the dry ingredients followed by half of the sour cream. Mix well on low speed. Repeat with remaining dry ingredients and sour cream.

Spread half of the batter into the prepared pan. Arrange the cherries evenly over the batter. Sprinkle with half of the streusel. Top with the remaining batter followed by the streusel.

Bake for 45 to 50 minutes or until toothpick inserted in center comes out clean. Let cool completely in pan before inverting cake. Place right-side up onto serving plate. Garnish with powdered sugar.

beach's best granola gv☀♥

Some days it takes me a while to physically get out of bed. On those days, I don't leave myself much time for breakfast. Luckily, I've devised a system where I can laze around in bed *and* have breakfast, all while being on time! My secret? Having breakfast ready to go on my way out the door and to the beach. This granola is the perfect make-ahead breakfast. Enjoy it as a cereal with milk, as a parfait with yogurt and fresh fruit, or as a heartier meal by mixing it with peanut butter and apple slices. This is also a recipe that begs for personalization. Feel free to add dried fruit or substitute different nuts when you try out this recipe. Any way you make it will be delicious and satisfying!

3 cups rolled oats

½ cup shredded sweetened coconut

½ cup sunflower seeds

½ cup almonds, chopped

¼ cup flax seeds

¼ cup light brown sugar

1 teaspoon pure vanilla extract

¼ teaspoon salt

⅓ cup olive oil

½ cup Grade A maple syrup

1 teaspoon ground cinnamon

1 Preheat the oven to 275 degrees. Line 2 cookie sheets with aluminum foil or parchment paper.

2 Combine the oats, coconut, sunflower seeds, almonds, flax seeds, brown sugar, vanilla, and salt in a medium stainless steel bowl.

3 Bring the olive oil, maple syrup, and cinnamon to boil in a small saucepan over high heat. Pour the hot liquid over the oat mixture and stir with a rubber spatula until all the oats and nuts are coated.

4 Divide the mixture between the 2 cookie sheets and spread out evenly.

5 Bake for 30 minutes. Stir the granola and bake 15 minutes more.

6 Remove the granola from the oven. Let it cool completely on the trays before storing in an air-tight container.

daybreak muffins ☀♥

Makes about 8 muffins

Crumb topping

½ cup light brown sugar

¼ cup all-purpose flour

1 teaspoon pure vanilla extract

½ teaspoon ground cinnamon

2 tablespoons unsalted butter, cold and cubed

Muffin

1¼ cups all-purpose flour

¼ cup oat bran

1 teaspoon baking soda

1 teaspoon baking powder

½ teaspoon salt

3 medium bananas, very ripe

1 large egg

½ cup sugar

⅓ cup unsalted butter, melted

½ teaspoon pure vanilla extract

As the sun peeks above the horizon and the first light of day hits your kitchen window, the aroma of these banana oat bran muffins baking in your oven will awaken your senses and get you jump started for the day ahead. Make sure to use oat bran (*not* oats) and very ripe bananas when making these muffins. You will find that they taste like the best bowl of oatmeal you've ever had or ever imagined having.

1 Preheat the oven to 375 degrees. Line a muffin pan with 8 paper liners.

2 *Make the crumb topping:* Combine all the ingredients in a medium bowl. Using your hands, rub the mixture between your fingers until it resembles coarse cornmeal. Place bowl in freezer while you make the muffin batter.

3 *Make the muffin batter:* In a large bowl, combine the flour, oat bran, baking soda, baking powder, and salt. In a separate bowl, mash the bananas with the back of a fork and whisk in the egg, sugar, butter, and vanilla. Stir in the flour mixture with a rubber spatula.

4 Scoop the batter into the paper liners, filling each one to the top. Remove crumb topping from the freezer. Sprinkle *half* of the topping onto each of the muffins, gently pressing the topping into the batter. Place the remaining crumb topping back into the freezer.

5 Bake muffins for 10 minutes. Remove from oven and sprinkle the remaining crumb topping over the muffins. Bake for an additional 8 to 10 minutes or until a toothpick comes out clean.

aged cheddar, bacon, and scallion biscuits

Makes 10 biscuits

My favorite cheddar cheese is by far Wisconsin aged cheddar, and I highly recommend using it in this insane biscuit. While most people associate Wisconsin with cheese more than beach-going, many beautiful beaches can in fact be found here. One such place is Kohler-Andrae State Park, which is home to more than two miles of golden "ocean-esque" beaches as well as the largest sand dune complex along Lake Michigan. Take a break from hiking nature trails and stake out a picnic spot along the sandy stretch of beach. Instead of rushing home at the end of the day, stay overnight at one of the many campsites throughout the park.

1 Preheat the oven to 425 degrees. Line a baking sheet with aluminum foil.

2 Shred the cheese and cold butter onto a large piece of plastic wrap. Wrap the mixture up with the plastic wrap and place it in the freezer to keep chilled.

3 Heat the oil in a sauté pan over medium heat. Add onions and cook until translucent, stirring occasionally. Add the sugar and continue cooking until browned and caramelized. This may take between 6 to 8 minutes. Stir occasionally to ensure even browning. Remove from heat and set aside.

4 In a large bowl, whisk together the flour, baking powder, salt, cooked onions, chopped bacon, and scallions. Work in the cold butter and cheese with your fingers quickly and gently. Make a well in the center. In a small bowl, whisk together the egg and buttermilk. Pour the egg mixture into the well. Mix the ingredients together with your hands until all ingredients are incorporated. Dough will be sticky. Using a large ice cream scoop (I use a 2½-ounce scoop), drop the biscuits onto the lined baking sheet. Allow at least a 1-inch space between the biscuits as they will expand when baking.

5 Bake for 14 to 15 minutes or until golden brown. Remove from the oven and brush with the melted butter. Best served warm.

4 ounces Wisconsin aged cheddar

6 tablespoons (¾ stick) unsalted butter, cold

1 tablespoon olive oil

1 small onion, diced (about 4 ounces)

2 tablespoons sugar

2 cups all-purpose flour

4 tablespoons baking powder

⅛ teaspoon salt

5 strips of bacon, cooked crispy and chopped into small pieces

⅓ cup chopped scallions, white and green parts (3 to 4 scallions)

1 large egg

1 cup buttermilk

¼ cup (½ stick) unsalted butter, melted

To reheat biscuits, simply place in a 350 degree oven for 10 minutes.

cranberry oat scones ♥☀

Makes 8 scones

2 cups rolled oats

1½ cups all-purpose flour

½ cup dried cranberries

½ cup sugar

4 teaspoons baking powder

½ teaspoon salt

1 large egg

½ cup unsalted butter, melted

½ cup buttermilk

1 teaspoon finely-grated orange zest

1 tablespoon sugar for sprinkling

Whenever I have these delicious, heart-warming scones, I always think of the beaches of Tofino, British Columbia, but it's not for the reason you suspect. During the days I spent in Tofino, the sky was dark, the wind was raging, waves were crashing, and the Pacific was spitting in every direction. Thankfully, I was able to watch the storms in the comfort and safety of a beautiful rustic lodge. That same coziness I felt there is what I've captured in these delicious scones. Winter storm watching in Tofino is a sight to behold and something everyone should experience at least once in their lifetime. It is a dramatic, mystical event as powerful tides change the landscape of the glorious beaches there every minute.

1 Preheat the oven to 400 degrees. Line a cookie sheet with aluminum foil or parchment paper.

2 In a large bowl, mix together the oats, flour, cranberries, sugar, baking powder, and salt. Make a well in the center. In a small bowl, beat the egg until frothy. Stir in the melted butter, buttermilk, and zest. Pour into the well, and mix with a rubber spatula to create a soft dough. Transfer dough to a lightly floured surface. Divide the dough in half and pat each portion into two circles, about 6-inches in diameter and ¾-inch thick. Cut 4 wedges into each circle of dough. Place on the prepared cookie sheet. Sprinkle the tops with sugar.

3 Bake for 18 to 20 minutes or until the tops of the scones bounce back when pressed gently. Let cool for at least 10 minutes before serving.

beachy beverages

Although this chapter doesn't involve any baking, I felt that this book would be incomplete without sharing some recipes for my favorite beach beverages. Beach weather can range from chilly, misty mornings to steaming hot afternoons to cool, breezy evenings. Therefore, beverages of all types, temperatures, and flavors play an important role for any beach loving person. I've gathered some of my favorite beverage recipes that can either accompany the sweet treats in this book or be enjoyed on their own.

ice cold lemonade gv⏰

Makes about 1 quart

1 cup water

½ cup sugar

2 tablespoons clover honey

12 ounces ice cubes, plus additional for serving

1½ cups freshly squeezed lemon juice (8 to 10 lemons)

1½ cups cold filtered water

1 lemon, sliced for garnishing and further flavoring

Nothing is more refreshing on a hot summer day than a tall glass of ice-cold lemonade. For those who like experimenting with different flavors, try adding herbs like rosemary to the sugar syrup before bringing to a boil.

1 Combine water, sugar, and honey in a small saucepan over high heat and bring to a rolling boil. Remove from heat and set aside.

2 Add the ice cubes, lemon juice, cold filtered water, and warm sugar syrup to blender. Process until completely smooth. Serve over additional ice cubes with lemon slices as garnish.

G's agave margaritas gv⏰

I'm fortunate to spend much of my time with G, someone who loves to eat and drink almost as much as I do. One of the meals we cherish most is our homemade tostadas. This dish is incomplete without a margarita and, after many attempts, we came up with this fine recipe for one of my favorite beach beverages.

1 Fill a cocktail shaker with ice cubes. Add the tequila, lime juice, and agave nectar. Cover and shake until mixed and chilled, about 30 seconds.

2 Run a lime slice around the edges of chilled rocks glasses. Pour some salt onto a small dish. Press the rim of the glasses into the salt to coat the edges.

3 Fill the glasses with ice. Pour the margarita over the ice.

Lots of ice cubes

1 cup of really good tequila (I prefer Herradura Reposado)

½ cup fresh lime juice (about 4 to 5 limes)

1 tablespoon agave nectar

Salt

tropical tea gv★

Makes about 1 quart

3 cups water

2 hibiscus tea bags *or* 4 grams of loose hibiscus tea

2 white tea bags *or* 4 grams of loose white tea

3 tablespoons agave nectar

2 grams fresh mint leaves (about 2 stems)

1 tray of ice cubes (about 10 ounces)

3 tablespoons fresh orange or tangerine juice

This all-natural tea is not only attractive to look at, it's also incredibly delicious and good for you. I enjoy sipping this refreshing tea on my late afternoon beach walks during the summer months. The delicate and subtle white tea serves as the perfect buffer to the tart hibiscus, while the orange juice and agave add the perfect amount of sweetness to round out this summertime beverage.

1 Bring the 3 cups of water to boil over high heat. Remove from the heat and add the teas, agave nectar, and torn mint leaves. Steep for 4 minutes.

2 Add the ice cubes to a tall pitcher. Strain the tea mixture over the ice. Add the orange juice.

3 Stir gently before pouring into tall glasses filled with ice. Garnish each glass with mint tops.

citrus and berry sangria gv★

Makes 750 milliliters

My Citrus and Berry Sangria is the perfect afternoon beverage on a hot summer day. As you can imagine, living by the beach I experience many hot summer days on which I enjoy this drink. Around the world, sangria is served most often in Spain and Portugal, the latter is home to the spectacular Algarve Coast. This southern-most region of Portugal is its most popular tourist destination with some 10 million visitors a year. While there, you should spend some time at Marinha Beach, considered by the Michelin Guide as one of the ten most beautiful beaches in Europe. With its stunning rock outcroppings and high cliffs, Marinha Beach is also known for the purity of its waters, unspoiled beauty, and sloping beaches.

1 (750ml) bottle of red wine (Zinfandels and Riojas work well)

8 ounces strawberries (12 to 14 medium strawberries)

1 large yellow peach

1 large Fuji apple

1 large naval orange

Handful of red grapes

½ cup blueberries

½ cup sugar

1 Place the red wine in the refrigerator to chill. Wash and pat dry all the fruit. Hull the strawberries and slice into quarters. Slice the peach, apple, and orange into small cubes and wedges.

2 Add the cut fruit including the grapes and blueberries to a large bowl. Sprinkle with sugar and toss to coat. Let the fruit marinate for 10 minutes.

3 Pour the red wine over the fruit and stir to combine thoroughly. Transfer to a tall pitcher for serving.

I like to use Dancing Bull Zinfandel 2011 in my Sangria.

fruit punch gv

Makes about 1 gallon

1 cup frozen lemon concentrate

2 cups frozen orange concentrate

1 cup sugar

1 cup water

2 cups pineapple juice

¼ cup lime juice (2 to 3 limes)

1 (12-ounce) can of ginger ale

1 lime, 1 orange, 1 lemon for garnish

This is a great beverage to serve at a large beach party when you have a hundred other things to worry about. It's embarrassingly easy to make, but the addition of fresh fruit adds a veil of disguise as being time consuming. Make a batch (or two) and serve it in a glass punch bowl. Place the bowl and ladle on your dining, kitchen, or picnic table and let your guests serve themselves so you can enjoy the party.

1 Let the lemon and orange concentrates thaw at room temperature while you make the simple syrup.

2 In a small saucepan, bring the sugar and water to a boil over high heat. Remove from the heat and set aside.

3 Add the lemon and orange concentrates to a large pot. Stir in the pineapple and lime juices. Pour the simple syrup over the juices and mix well. Stir in the ginger ale.

4 Cut thin slices of the lime, orange, and lemon and place into a large punch bowl or pitcher. Pour the punch over the fruit.

BEACH HOUSE BAKING
★ 28 ★

the best hot cocoa

Makes 4 cups

1¼ cups (8 ounces) milk chocolate, chopped

½ cup heavy cream

3 cups whole milk

Whipped cream, marshmallows, cinnamon for garnish (optional)

The key to making exceptional hot chocolate is blending chocolate ganache with warm whole milk. The ganache may be made ahead and stored in the refrigerator so you can have hot cocoa anytime you crave it. And the best part is . . . no sugar needed!

1 Placed the chopped chocolate in a small bowl and set aside.

2 Add the heavy cream to a medium saucepan and bring to a simmer over medium heat. Remove from heat, add the chocolate into the hot cream, and let sit for 1 minute before whisking until blended. Transfer the ganache to a bowl and set aside.

3 In the same saucepan, warm up the milk over medium heat. When bubbles begin forming on the edges, whisk in the ganache. Pour the hot cocoa into mugs and top with whipped cream, marshmallows, or cinnamon, if desired.

On warmer days, add a shot of espresso to your hot chocolate and enjoy it over ice. It's delicious!

surfer cowboy coffee gv⏰

Makes just over 4 cups

If you decide to hit the waves at the crack of dawn, you have to be *very* awake. If there isn't a coffee shop open during those early hours, you may need to go old-school and make coffee at the beach (hopefully, the beach allows campfires). Once you get a small fire going, grab a pot out of your jeep and fill it with a couple bottles of water. Toss in the coffee grounds, and in two minutes you'll have the original energy drink ready to go.

4¼ cups filtered water

⅓ cup finely ground coffee

1 Fill a medium pot with 4 cups of filtered water. Add the coffee grounds to the water. Do not stir in.

2 Place the pot over medium-high heat and bring just to a rolling boil.

3 Remove from the heat. Splash the remaining ¼ cup of water over the coffee.

4 Let the coffee sit 1 minute to settle the grounds. Pour into your mug and enjoy!

coconut chai tea latte 9★

Makes 3 cups (2 servings)

5 cardamom pods

5 whole cloves

1 (2-inch) cinnamon stick, broken in half

1-inch piece of fresh ginger, peeled and sliced

2 cups filtered water

1 tablespoon clover honey

2 black tea bags *or* 4 grams of loose black tea

½ cup whole or 2-percent milk

½ cup unsweetened coconut milk

Living so close to the beach, I often wake up to a cool marine layer hovering over the beach house. Instead of turning on the heat, I sip this soothing latte to warm up my toes. So when you feel a chill in the air, make this amazing tea, find a warm corner, and let your temperature rise.

1 Grind the cardamom pods, cloves, cinnamon stick, and ginger slices with a mortar and pestle. Add the mixture to a small saucepan and fill with 2 cups filtered water. Place over high heat and bring the water to a rolling boil. Remove from the heat and stir in the honey and tea. Let steep for 4 minutes.

2 While the tea is steeping, combine the milks in a medium saucepan and bring to a low rolling boil. Pour the milk into the tea mixture. Strain the tea into 2 mugs.

cupcakes

Cupcakes are by far the most popular treat at Sugar Blossom, my beach town bake shop in San Clemente. The cupcake's individual serving and dainty appearance make it an attractive option to those wanting to celebrate without the fuss of utensils; to those looking to transport them and celebrate a distance away; to those looking to present a small gift to cheer up a sad friend; as well as to those who just need to satisfy a sweet craving without feeling guilty.

The cupcake recipes in this chapter are some of my favorites. They range from classic **Vanilla** (page 38) and **Dark Chocolate** (page 41) to more sophisticated specialties such as **"Light as a Kite" Lemon Meringue** (page 48) and **Banana Pecan with Honey Buttercream** (page 56). My goal was to create delicious takes on the classics and a few new out-of-the-box twists.

At the time of this writing, the cupcake still reigns at the top. Though we say we're ready for the next big sweet treat, we're secretly cheering you on, cupcake! You've brought us a lot of joy and pleasure . . . we'll ignore those few extra pounds.

golden butter cupcakes with madagascar vanilla buttercream

Makes about 20 cupcakes

Cupcakes
2 cups cake flour
2½ teaspoons baking powder
¾ teaspoon salt
¾ cup (1½ sticks) unsalted butter, at room temperature
1½ cups sugar
1½ teaspoons pure vanilla extract
3 large eggs
¾ cup whole milk

Madagascar Vanilla Buttercream
5 cups powdered sugar
2 cups (4 sticks) unsalted butter, at room temperature
1½ tablespoons whole milk
1 teaspoon pure vanilla extract
⅛ teaspoon salt

Make homemade vanilla extract by soaking 2 scraped vanilla beans in a cup of vodka in a glass jar with lid. Allow the mixture to infuse in a cool, dark place at least 1 month before using. Make sure to shake the mixture once a week.

This delicious cupcake highlights the delicate floral flavor of vanilla. I recommend using Madagascar vanilla for its purity and depth of flavor. Madagascar is an island country in the Indian Ocean that is home to the most popular and sought after vanilla in the world. The vanilla beans grown here are plump, moist, and bursting with aromatics that put other vanilla to shame. The tropical climate of Madagascar is the perfect environment for producing this treasured baking ingredient . . . and yes, you guessed it, for sun bathing. With 1800 miles of palm-fringed coastline, Madagascar will be steps away with one bite of these namesake cupcakes.

1 Preheat the oven to 350 degrees. Line cupcake pans with 20 paper liners.

2 Sift the cake flour, baking powder, and salt. Set aside.

3 In a mixer fitted with the paddle attachment, cream the butter, sugar, and vanilla on medium speed until light and fluffy, about 2 minutes. Mix in the eggs one at a time, scraping well after each addition. With the mixer on low speed, add the milk and flour mixture alternately, beginning with the milk and ending with the flour.

4 Scoop the batter into the cupcake liners, filling them just below the rim. (I use a 2-ounce ice cream scoop.) Bake in the center of the oven for 17 to 18 minutes or until a toothpick comes out clean. Cool for 10 minutes, remove from the pans, and allow to cool completely before frosting.

5 *Make the frosting:* Sift the powdered sugar and set aside.

In a mixer fitted with the paddle attachment, cream the butter on medium speed until very smooth and soft. Add the sifted powdered sugar to the butter and mix on low speed until incorporated. Add in the milk, vanilla extract, and salt. Mix on medium speed for 2 minutes to ensure that the frosting is light and fluffy.

dark chocolate cupcakes with creamy chocolate frosting

Makes about 12 cupcakes

The highest quality cocoa bean is known as Criollo. One of the largest producers of the Criollo bean is Venezuela, also home to the longest stretch of Caribbean coastline of any country in the Americas. Most beach-goers flock to the shallow blue waters and white sand beaches of Margarita Island, about 25 miles from the mainland. Affectionately called the Pearl of the Caribbean, Margarita Island provides a true tropical beach vacation. Best part of it all? The three main cities on the island offer numerous lodging right on the sand so you will be at the beach at all times.

1 Preheat the oven to 375 degrees. Line a cupcake pan with 12 paper liners.

2 Sift the cake flour, cocoa powder, baking powder, baking soda, and salt. Set aside.

3 In a mixer fitted with the paddle attachment, cream the butter and sugar until light and fluffy, about 1 minute. Add the eggs one at a time, scraping well after each addition. With the mixer on low speed, add the milk and flour mixture alternately, beginning with the milk and ending with the flour. Scrape the bowl well to make sure all the ingredients are incorporated.

4 Scoop the batter into the cupcake liners, filling them just below the rim. (I use a 2-ounce ice cream scoop.) Bake in the center of the oven for 14 to 15 minutes or until a toothpick comes out clean. Cool for 10 minutes, remove from the pans, and allow to cool completely before frosting.

5 *Make the frosting:* Sift the powdered sugar and cocoa powder. Set aside.

In a mixer fitted with the paddle attachment, beat the butter on medium speed until very smooth. Add about 1 cup of the powdered sugar mixture alternately with 2 tablespoons of evaporated milk. Repeat step until all the powdered sugar and milk are added. Blend in the vanilla extract. Mix on medium speed for 2 minutes to ensure that the frosting is light and fluffy.

Cupcakes

¾ cup cake flour

½ cup unsweetened dark cocoa powder (I recommend Cacao Barry Extra Brute)

½ teaspoon baking powder

¼ teaspoon baking soda

⅛ teaspoon salt

½ cup (1 stick) unsalted butter, at room temperature

1¼ cups sugar

2 large eggs

½ cup whole milk, warmed slightly

Creamy Chocolate Frosting

5½ cups powdered sugar

¾ cup unsweetened dark cocoa powder (I recommend Cacao Barry Extra Brute)

¾ cup (1½ sticks) unsalted butter, at room temperature

1 (5-ounce) can evaporated milk

1 teaspoon pure vanilla extract

I have found that while there are many brands of cocoa powder available, there are certain ones that are far superior in flavor such as Cacao Barry, Valrhona, and Scharffenberger. These brands can be found at specialty food stores.

s'mores cupcakes ★ ☼

Makes about 23 cupcakes

Graham Crust

1⅛ cups graham crumbs

¼ cup sugar

3 tablespoons unsalted butter, melted

S'more Batter

1 cup cake flour

1½ teaspoons baking powder

1 teaspoon baking soda

½ teaspoon salt

½ cup (1 stick) unsalted butter, at room temperature

1 cup light brown sugar

1 large egg

1 teaspoon pure vanilla extract

1½ ounces semi-sweet chocolate, melted

¼ cup plain yogurt

½ cup boiling water

207 mini marshmallows

Ganache

¾ cup dark chocolate, chopped

½ cup heavy cream

Powdered sugar for garnish

As the sun sets in north San Diego County, dots of fire light up the early evening sky all along the beaches of San Onofre State Park. Here, surfers gather around fire pits sharing highlights of their day at Trestles, the world renowned surfing beach and home to the annual ASP World Surfing competition. Graham crackers, chocolate bars, and jumbo marshmallows get passed around the fire and soon the scent of toasted marshmallow and melted chocolate fills the air. As the sun disappears, silhouettes of figures eating this classic campfire treat are all that can be seen between tall sandstone bluffs on one side and the waves of the Pacific on the other.

1 Preheat the oven to 375 degrees. Line a cupcake pan with 23 paper liners.

2 Combine the graham crumbs and sugar in a medium bowl. Mix in the melted butter with your hands. Place 1 tablespoon of the mixture into each cupcake liner. Pat down with the back of an ice cream scoop handle.

3 Sift the cake flour, baking powder, baking soda, and salt. Set aside.

4 In a mixer fitted with the paddle attachment, cream the butter and brown sugar until light and fluffy, about 2 minutes. Add the egg and vanilla, and mix until combined. Scrape bowl well. Mix in the melted chocolate on low speed. Add the dry ingredients and the yogurt. Mix for 1 minute on low speed. Pour in the boiling water all at once and mix just until combined. Scrape the bowl well to make sure all the ingredients are incorporated. Batter will be runny.

5 Immediately pour the batter into the prepared cupcake liners, filling them *halfway*. Batter will rise up considerably when baked. Top each cupcake with nine mini marshmallows in rows of 3 by 3. Bake in the center of the oven for 17 to 18 minutes or until a toothpick comes out clean. Cool for 10 minutes, remove from the pan, and place on wire rack to cool completely while you make the ganache.

6 *Make the ganache:* Place the chopped chocolate in a medium heat-proof bowl. Bring the heavy cream to a boil in a saucepan over medium high heat. Remove from heat and pour over the chocolate. Let sit for 1 minute. Whisk the cream into the chocolate until smooth and silky.

7 Drizzle each cupcake with warm ganache and top with powdered sugar before serving.

german chocolate getaway

Makes about 10 cupcakes

Here's an example of how far imagination can take you. What do you think is inside the largest freestanding building in the world? Aircraft production? Shipbuilding? Oh no, my friends—it's a beach. It's an indoor tropical paradise that includes a rainforest, a waterfall, and pools with waterslides all kept at a constant temperature of 78 degrees. Believe it or not, this fantastical place is an actual resort called Tropical Islands Resort and is located in Krausnick, south of Berlin. Built in 2004, this dome-shaped resort was constructed in a former aircraft hangar and can easily fit eight football fields. Now that's a lot of beach!

1 Preheat the oven to 375 degrees. Line the cupcake pans with 10 paper liners.

2 Place chopped chocolate in a microwave-safe bowl. Melt until smooth. Set aside.

3 Sift the cake flour, baking soda, and salt. Set aside.

4 In a mixer fitted with the whip attachment, whip the egg whites to medium peak on high speed. Transfer the whipped whites to a clean bowl and set them aside.

5 In the same mixing bowl, cream the butter, sugar, and vanilla extract with the paddle attachment until light and fluffy, about 2 minutes. Add the yolks one at a time, scraping well after each addition. Blend in the melted chocolate on low speed. Make sure to scrape the sides of the bowl well. Add the buttermilk alternately with the dry ingredients, beginning with the buttermilk and ending with the flour. Remove

bowl from mixer. Using a rubber spatula, fold in the 2 tablespoons of hot water followed by the whipped whites.

6 Scoop the batter into the cupcake liners, filling them just below the rim. (I use a 2-ounce ice cream scoop.) Bake in the center of the oven for 14 to 15 minutes or until a toothpick comes out clean. Cool for 10 minutes, remove from the pans, and allow to cool completely before frosting.

7 *Make the frosting:* Combine first 5 ingredients in a medium saucepan. Stirring constantly, cook the mixture over medium heat until bubbly and thickened (you may need to switch between using a whisk and a rubber spatula). Make sure to boil for at least 1 minute to thicken mixture. Remove from the heat and stir in the coconut and pecans. Transfer the mixture to a container, place in the refrigerator uncovered, and allow to cool completely before using.

Cupcakes
2 ounces German sweet chocolate, chopped

1⅛ cups cake flour

¾ teaspoon baking soda

⅛ teaspoon salt

2 large eggs, separated

½ cup (1 stick) unsalted butter, at room temperature

1 cup sugar

½ teaspoon pure vanilla extract

½ cup buttermilk

2 tablespoons hot water

Coconut Pecan Frosting
1 (12-ounce) can evaporated milk

6 large egg yolks

2 cups sugar

1 cup (2 sticks) unsalted butter, at room temperature

2 teaspoons pure vanilla extract

4 cups shredded sweetened coconut

2 cups pecans, chopped

Did you know German chocolate actually has no ties to Germany? Rather, it is named after its creator, Samuel German, who in 1852 developed this "pre-sweetened" chocolate for bakers to use.

red velvet riviera

Makes about 16 cupcakes

Cupcakes

2 cups cake flour

1 teaspoon baking powder

1 teaspoon salt

2 tablespoons unsweetened cocoa powder

2 ounces red food coloring

½ cup (1 stick) unsalted butter, at room temperature

1½ cups sugar

2 large eggs

1 teaspoon pure vanilla extract

1 cup buttermilk

1 teaspoon distilled white vinegar

1 teaspoon baking soda

Vanilla Cream Cheese Frosting

3½ cups powdered sugar

1 pound cream cheese, cold

½ cup (1 stick) unsalted butter, at room temperature

1 teaspoon pure vanilla extract

Maui is one of the most beautiful places I have ever been. Luckily for me, I frequently get to go there. How, you ask? Well, multiple times a week I find myself making red velvet cupcakes at Sugar Blossom. The deep crimson red of this spongy cake always takes me back to the red sand beach of Kaihalulu Bay. This hidden cove is so beautiful and worth the short, but somewhat treacherous hike to get there. Here, the coastline is complemented with the bluest of water and surrounded by dramatic cliffs of lava rock.

1 Preheat the oven to 350 degrees. Line the cupcake pans with 16 paper liners.

2 Sift the cake flour, baking powder, and salt. Set aside.

3 In a small bowl, whisk together the cocoa powder and red food color. Set aside.

4 In a mixer fitted with the paddle attachment, cream the butter and sugar for about 3 minutes until fluffy. Add eggs one at a time. Make sure to scrape the bowl well after each addition. Stir in the vanilla.

5 Add flour mixture alternately with buttermilk, beginning with the buttermilk and ending with the dry ingredients. Add the food color mixture and mix on low speed just until uniform color is achieved. Make sure to scrape the bowl well.

6 In a small bowl, mix the vinegar with baking soda. The mixture will bubble. Fold this liquid into the cake batter with a rubber spatula.

7 Scoop the batter into the cupcake liners, filling them just below the rim. (I use a 2-ounce ice cream scoop.) Bake in the center of the oven for 13 to 15 minutes or until a toothpick comes out clean. Cool for 10 minutes, remove from the pans, and allow to cool completely before frosting.

8 *Make the frosting:* Sift the powdered sugar and set aside.

In a mixer fitted with the paddle attachment, beat the cream cheese, butter, and vanilla on medium speed until blended. Scrape down the sides of the bowl well and mix for another 2 minutes to ensure no lumps remain.

Add the powdered sugar all at once and beat on low speed just until sugar is incorporated. Then beat at high speed for 10 seconds. Scrape down sides well. Beat the mixture again on high speed for 10 seconds.

"light as a kite" lemon meringue cupcakes ★

Makes about 16 cupcakes

Lemon Custard

½ cup (1 stick) unsalted butter, at room temperature

7 tablespoons sugar

3 tablespoons lemon juice

1 teaspoon finely grated lemon zest

5 large egg yolks

Lemon Cupcakes

1¾ cups cake flour

¾ teaspoon baking soda

½ teaspoon salt

3 large eggs, separated

¾ cup (1½ sticks) unsalted butter, at room temperature

1 cup sugar

½ teaspoon pure lemon extract

½ teaspoon finely grated lemon zest

½ cup buttermilk

2 tablespoons distilled white vinegar

Lemon Meringue

½ cup cold water

12 tablespoons sugar

2 tablespoons meringue powder

½ teaspoon pure lemon extract

Another image of summer that reminds me of warm days and gentle breezes is families running along the sand working hard to get their kites up in the air, making sure each kite has just the right length of tail to make it soar. Once they finally catch a breeze, it's magical to watch the colorful shapes climb rapidly to the sky. I created these lemon cupcakes to capture that lighter-than-air feeling.

1 *Make the custard:* Combine *half* of the butter, 4 tablespoons sugar, lemon juice, and zest in a medium saucepan. Bring to a boil over medium heat, stirring occasionally.

Meanwhile, whisk the egg yolks and the remaining 3 tablespoons sugar in a small bowl. Slowly add half of the hot lemon juice mixture to the yolks, whisking constantly.

Return the tempered egg mixture to the saucepan over low-medium heat. Continue cooking, stirring constantly, until the custard boils for 10 seconds. Remove from heat and strain into a shallow container or bowl.

Stir in the remaining butter and press plastic wrap directly onto the surface of the custard. Place in refrigerator to cool while you make the cupcakes.

2 *Make the cupcakes:* Preheat the oven to 350 degrees. Line cupcake pans with 16 paper liners.

Sift the cake flour, baking soda, and salt. Set aside.

In a mixer fitted with the whip attachment, whip the eggs whites to medium peak. Transfer the whipped whites to a clean bowl and set them aside.

Add the butter, sugar, lemon extract, and zest to the mixing bowl and mix on medium speed until light and fluffy, about 2 minutes. Mix in the yolks one at a time, scraping well after each addition. Combine the buttermilk and vinegar in a small cup and stir gently. With the mixer on low speed, add the buttermilk mixture and flour alternately, beginning with the liquids and ending with the flour. Fold in the egg whites with a rubber spatula.

Scoop the batter into the cupcake liners. (I use a 2-ounce ice cream scoop.) Bake in the center of the oven for 18 to 20 minutes or until a toothpick comes out clean. Cool for 10 minutes, remove from the pans and allow to cool completely before frosting.

Carve out the center of each cooled cupcake. Pipe or spoon the lemon custard into each center. Set aside while you make the meringue.

3 *Make the meringue:* In a mixer fitted with the whip attachment, combine water, 6 tablespoons of the sugar, meringue powder, and the lemon extract. Whip on high for 3 minutes. Add the remaining sugar. Whip for 2 more minutes until thick, glossy, and fluffy. Use immediately and torch as desired.

surfin' P.B.J.

Makes about 10 cupcakes

This recipe packs memories of childhood in one sweet cupcake. Jelly is piped into the center of a chocolate peanut butter cupcake so every bite contains peanut butter *and* jelly!

1 Preheat the oven to 350 degrees. Line the cupcake pans with 10 paper liners.

2 Sift the cake flour, cocoa powder, baking soda, and salt. Set aside.

3 In a mixer fitted with the paddle attachment, cream the butter, peanut butter, and sugar on medium speed until light and fluffy, about 2 minutes. Add the egg and vanilla and mix until incorporated. In a small bowl, whisk together the half-and-half with the sour cream. With the mixer on low speed, add the sour cream mixture and flour mixture alternately, beginning with the wet and ending with the dry. Scrape the bowl well to make sure all the ingredients are incorporated.

4 Scoop the batter into the cupcake liners, filling them just below the rim. (I use a 2-ounce ice cream scoop.) Bake in the center of the oven for 15 to 17 minutes or until a toothpick comes out clean. Cool for 10 minutes, remove from the pans, and allow to cool completely before frosting.

5 Carve out the center of each cooled cupcake. Pipe or spoon jelly into each center. Frost with peanut butter frosting.

6 *Make the frosting:* In a mixer fitted with the paddle attachment, mix the peanut butter and butter on medium speed until smooth. Add the powdered sugar, milk, vanilla, and salt. Mix on low speed until incorporated. Increase to medium speed and mix until light and fluffy, about 2 minutes.

Cupcakes

1 cup cake flour

¼ cup unsweetened cocoa powder

1 teaspoon baking soda

¼ teaspoon salt

¼ cup (½ stick) unsalted butter, at room temperature

¼ cup smooth peanut butter

¾ cup sugar

1 large egg

½ teaspoon pure vanilla extract

½ cup sour cream

½ cup half-and-half

1 cup of your favorite jelly

Peanut Butter Frosting

1½ cups smooth peanut butter

¾ cup (1½ sticks) unsalted butter, at room temperature

2 cups powdered sugar, sifted

2 tablespoons whole milk

1 teaspoon pure vanilla extract

⅛ teaspoon salt

tropical carrot cupcakes with ginger frosting

Makes about 12 cupcakes

Cupcakes

1 cup cake flour

1 teaspoon baking powder

½ teaspoon baking soda

½ teaspoon salt

¼ teaspoon ground cinnamon

2 large eggs

¾ cup sugar

¾ cup canola oil

1 teaspoon pure vanilla extract

1 teaspoon finely grated orange zest

1 cup shredded carrots

½ cup crushed pineapple, drained

⅓ cup shredded sweetened coconut

Ginger Frosting

2⅔ cups powdered sugar

8 ounces cream cheese, cold

6 tablespoons (¾ stick) unsalted butter, at room temperature

2 teaspoons finely grated peeled fresh ginger

When I began developing these cupcakes, I was inspired by the classic carrot cake, a long-time favorite of mine. I wanted to make it more tropical so I decided to pack it with vanilla, citrus, coconut, and juicy pineapple. These cupcakes always put me in a tropical mood and when I think of tropical, I think of the colorful birds I have seen in the Costa Rican rainforests of Manuel Antonio National Park. The bird watching tours there ensure that visitors see the hundreds of species of tropical birds that inhabit the park. This beautiful park also happens to include numerous hidden beaches where you can watch breathtaking sunsets after a day of bird watching.

1 Preheat the oven to 350 degrees. Line the cupcake pan with 12 paper liners.

2 Sift the cake flour, baking powder, baking soda, salt, and cinnamon. Set aside.

3 In a large bowl, vigorously whisk the eggs, sugar, canola oil, vanilla, and zest for 1 minute. Stir in the carrots, pineapple, and coconut with a rubber spatula. Stir in flour mixture until incorporated.

4 Scoop the batter into the cupcake liners, filling them just below the rim. (I use a 2-ounce ice cream scoop.) Bake in the center of the oven for 15 to 17 minutes or until a toothpick comes out clean. Cool for 10 minutes, remove from the pans, and allow to cool completely before frosting.

5 *Make the frosting:* Sift the powdered sugar and set aside.

In a mixer fitted with the paddle attachment, beat the cream cheese, butter, and ginger on medium speed until blended. Scrape down the sides of the bowl well and mix for another 2 minutes to ensure no lumps remain.

Add the powdered sugar all at once and beat on low speed just until sugar is incorporated. Then beat at high speed for 10 seconds. Scrape down sides well. Beat the mixture again on high speed for 10 seconds.

moist pumpkin cupcakes
with maple cinnamon frosting and slightly sweetened pepitas

Makes about 11 cupcakes

While driving cross country last year, I stopped in Peoria, Illinois, surrounded by pumpkin patches. The area in and around Peoria cultivates most pumpkins grown in the United States. After pumpkin patch hopping, I drove to Chicago along Lake Michigan where I was greeted by yet another surprise: a beach. Many people don't realize that along the twenty-six miles of shoreline are several public beaches and waterfront areas. One of my favorites was Oak Street Beach. It's located at the northern end of Michigan Avenue, making it the perfect way to end a day of shopping and sightseeing.

1 *Make the cupcakes:* Preheat the oven to 350 degrees. Line the cupcake pan with 11 paper liners.

Sift the cake flour, apple pie spice, baking powder, baking soda, and salt. Set aside.

In a large bowl, whisk together the eggs, pumpkin, sugars, and melted butter for 1 minute. Whisk in the flour mixture until all ingredients are incorporated.

Scoop the batter into the cupcake liners, filling them just below the rim. (I use a 2-ounce ice cream scoop.) Bake in the center of the oven for 20 to 22 minutes or until a toothpick comes out clean. Cool for 10 minutes, remove from the pans and allow to cool completely before frosting and garnishing with pepitas.

2 *Make the pepitas:* Preheat oven to 350 degrees. Line a baking tray with aluminum foil or parchment paper.

Place pepitas in a medium bowl. In a small cup, dissolve the sugar in the water. Pour over pepitas and toss to coat. Spread out onto prepared baking tray.

Bake for 8 to 10 minutes or until seeds are lightly browned and puffed. Remove from oven and let cool completely on tray.

3 *Make the frosting:* Sift the powdered sugar and set aside.

In a mixer fitted with the paddle attachment, beat the cream cheese, butter, maple syrup, and cinnamon on medium speed until blended. Scrape down the sides of the bowl well and mix for another 2 minutes to ensure no lumps remain.

Add the powdered sugar all at once and beat on low speed just until sugar is incorporated. Then beat at high speed for 10 seconds. Scrape down sides well. Beat the mixture again on high speed for 10 seconds.

Cupcakes

1 cup cake flour

1 teaspoon apple pie spice

¾ teaspoon baking powder

½ teaspoon baking soda

½ teaspoon salt

2 large eggs

1 cup canned pure pumpkin

½ cup sugar

½ cup light brown sugar, packed

½ cup (1 stick) unsalted butter, melted

Slightly Sweetened Pepitas

½ cup raw pepitas

1 teaspoon sugar

1 teaspoon hot tap water

Maple Cinnamon Frosting

2 cups powdered sugar

6 ounces cream cheese, cold

5 tablespoons unsalted butter, at room temperature

2 tablespoons Grade A maple syrup

½ teaspoon ground cinnamon

banana pecan cupcakes with honey buttercream ★

Makes about 14 cupcakes

Cupcakes

¾ cup (about 2 medium) bananas, very ripe

1½ cups cake flour

¾ teaspoon baking soda

⅛ teaspoon salt

½ cup (1 stick) unsalted butter, at room temperature

¾ cup sugar

1 large egg

1 teaspoon pure vanilla extract

¾ cup buttermilk

½ cup pecans, chopped into small pieces

Honey Buttercream

3½ cups powdered sugar, sifted

1 cup (2 sticks) unsalted butter, at room temperature

¼ cup clover honey

¼ cup sour cream

These cupcakes are best made with very ripe bananas so plan ahead and place yellow bananas in a brown paper bag for a few days before making this recipe. When you open the bag, get ready to head to Central America. You can find banana farms everywhere in Central America, a destination for many who long for the relaxed surfer lifestyle this region offers. In the southwest corner of Nicaragua lies the off-the-grid surfer haven of Popoyo. Located three hours from Managua, the capital of Nicaragua, Popoyo is the hidden gem of this country. Here you will find uncrowded beaches, epic surf breaks, and spearfishing hotspots. If you're looking for a trip that will leave you relaxed, sunburnt, exhilarated, exhausted, *and* achy, Popoyo is the place to go.

1 Preheat the oven to 350 degrees. Line the cupcake pan with 14 paper liners.

2 In a small bowl, mash the bananas with a fork and set aside.

3 Sift the flour, baking soda, and salt. Set aside.

4 In a mixer fitted with the paddle attachment, cream the butter and sugar on medium speed for about 3 minutes until fluffy. Add egg and vanilla and mix for 1 minute. Scrape the bowl well. Add flour mixture alternately with the buttermilk, beginning with the buttermilk and ending with the flour. Fold in the mashed bananas and pecan pieces with a rubber spatula.

5 Scoop the batter into the cupcake liners, filling them just below the rim. (I use a 2-ounce ice cream scoop.) Bake in the center of the oven for 15 to 17 minutes, until a toothpick comes out clean. Cool for 10 minutes, remove from the pans, and allow to cool completely before frosting.

6 *Make the frosting:* In a mixer fitted with the paddle attachment, beat all ingredients on low speed for 1 minute. Increase to medium speed and beat for 2 to 3 more minutes until smooth.

happy hour cupcakes

Legend has it that the term *happy hour* originated in the US Navy when sailors were given an hour to relieve the stress of a long deployment at sea. These days, it has come to be known as a time when establishments lower the prices of adult beverages in the late afternoon so people can relax after a hard day. I decided this same desire to relax should be embodied in something baked and delicious. So I've created some cupcake recipes that include some of my favorite adult beverages. I hope these bring you many, many hours of happiness.

jamaican rum cupcakes with spiced whipped cream frosting

Makes about 8 cupcakes

Cupcakes
1 cup cake flour
½ teaspoon baking powder
¼ teaspoon baking soda
½ cup shredded sweetened coconut
½ teaspoon ground cinnamon
¼ teaspoon ground ginger
¼ teaspoon ground nutmeg
¼ teaspoon ground cloves
⅛ teaspoon salt
½ cup (1 stick) unsalted butter, room temperature
½ cup sugar
1 teaspoon molasses
½ teaspoon pure vanilla extract
1 large egg
¼ cup half-and-half
¼ cup Appleton Jamaican rum

Garnish
1 cup shredded sweetened coconut

Spiced Whipped Cream Frosting
1½ cups heavy cream, chilled
1 tablespoon sugar
½ teaspoon ground cinnamon

On the northern coast of Jamaica, just under two hours from Montego Bay, lies Ochos Rios. Spend your day sunbathing on white sand beaches and soaking in the lush beauty of the Jamaican coastline. During the night, there are numerous bars where you can enjoy live reggae music while sipping Jamaican rum and enjoying the flavorful and spicy cuisine of the island. A fun excursion while in Ochos Rios is Dunn's River Falls. Here you can climb up terraced limestone "stairs" while cool mountain waters plunge above (and on) you.

1 Preheat the oven to 350 degrees. Line the cupcake pan with 8 liners and set aside.

2 Sift the flour, baking powder, and baking soda. Add the coconut, spices, and salt to the dry ingredients and set aside.

3 In a mixer fitted with the paddle attachment, cream the butter, sugar, molasses, and vanilla extract on medium speed for about 2 minutes until light and fluffy. Add egg and mix for an additional minute. Make sure to scrape the bowl well to ensure ingredients are incorporated. Add the flour mixture alternately with the half-and-half and rum, beginning with the liquids and ending with the flour.

4 Scoop the batter into the cupcake liners, filling them just below the rim. (Use a 2-ounce ice cream scoop.) Bake in the center of the oven for 17 to 19 minutes, or until a toothpick comes out clean. Cool for 10 minutes, remove from the pans and allow to cool completely before frosting and garnishing with toasted coconut.

5 *Make the garnish:* Place shredded coconut in a large skillet. Cook over medium heat, stirring frequently until the flakes are evenly golden brown. Transfer to a plate to cool completely.

6 *Make the frosting:* In a mixer fitted with the whip attachment, mix the cream, sugar, and cinnamon on high speed to medium-stiff peaks.

pint o' guinness cupcakes

Makes about 10 cupcakes

This cupcake was developed as a special at Sugar Blossom for St. Patrick's Day. It sold so well we now bring it back several times a year. The Guinness in the cupcake as well as in the meringue topping makes this happy hour cupcake doubly delicious!

1 Preheat oven to 400 degrees. Line a cupcake pan with 10 liners.

2 Sift together the flour and baking soda. Set aside.

3 In a medium saucepan, warm the Guinness and butter over low heat until the butter is melted. Remove from heat and whisk in the sugar and cocoa powder. In a separate bowl, whisk the sour cream and egg. Add mixture to saucepan and mix well. Gently whisk in the flour mixture until all the flour is incorporated. Batter will be runny.

4 Scoop the batter into the cupcake liners about three-quarters full. (I use a 2-ounce ice cream scoop.) Bake in the center of the oven for 12 to 13 minutes or until a toothpick comes out clean. Cool for 10 minutes, remove from the pans, and allow to cool completely before frosting.

5 *Make the meringue:* In a mixer fitted with the whip attachment, combine 3 tablespoons of the sugar, meringue powder, Guinness, and water. Whip on high speed for 3 minutes. Add the remaining sugar and whip on high for an additional 2 minutes. Use immediately and torch as desired.

Cupcakes

1 cup cake flour

1¼ teaspoons baking soda

½ cup Guinness

5 tablespoons unsalted butter

1 cup sugar

2 tablespoons unsweetened cocoa powder

⅓ cup sour cream

1 large egg

Guinness Meringue

6 tablespoons sugar

4½ teaspoons meringue powder

4½ teaspoons Guinness

1 tablespoon cold water

red, red wine cupcakes with blackberry mascarpone mousse *

Makes about 8 cupcakes

Cupcakes

1 cup cake flour

3 tablespoons unsweetened cocoa powder

½ teaspoon baking soda

½ cup (1 stick) unsalted butter, at room temperature

½ cup sugar

¼ teaspoon pure vanilla extract

¼ teaspoon pure almond extract

1 large egg

½ cup good red wine

Blackberry Mascarpone Mousse

½ cup ripe blackberries

2 cups mascarpone cheese

⅔ cup heavy cream, chilled

½ cup sugar

I love this cupcake because of the complex flavors that are transferred from the wine to the cake. I prefer cabernet wine with black-fruit aromatics, but feel free to experiment with other types of red wine. It's worth splurging on a nice bottle of red as you will have a lot left over to enjoy on its own.

1 Preheat oven to 350 degrees. Line a cupcake pan with 8 liners.

2 Sift together flour, cocoa powder, and baking soda. Set aside.

3 In a mixer fitted with the paddle attachment, cream the butter, sugar, and extracts on medium speed until light and fluffy, about 1 minute. Mix in egg until incorporated. Mix in the dry ingredients alternately with the red wine, beginning with the wine and ending with the flour. Do not over mix.

4 Scoop the batter into the cupcake liners, about three-quarters full. (I use a 2-ounce ice cream scoop.) Bake in the center of the oven for 15 to 17 minutes or until a toothpick comes out clean. Cool for 10 minutes, remove from the pans, and allow to cool completely before frosting.

5 *Make the mousse:* Mash the blackberries with a mortar and pestle. In a mixer fitted with the whip attachment, combine the blackberries, mascarpone, heavy cream, and sugar. Mix on medium-high speed until thickened, about 2 minutes. Use immediately.

PCH (piña colada highway) cupcakes

Makes about 14 cupcakes

This cupcake was inspired by a trip my girlfriends and I took to Puerto Rico, where rum is plentiful. The cake is super flavorful thanks to the rum and coconut milk in the batter. The "piña" is in the form of a caramelized baby pineapple ring that is crowned with a striking maraschino cherry. Every time I have these cupcakes, I recall sipping piña coladas under the shade of an umbrella with my feet buried beneath warm sand.

1 *Make the cupcake:* Preheat oven to 350 degrees. Line cupcake pan with 14 liners.

Sift flour, baking powder, baking soda, and salt. Set aside.

In a mixer fitted with the paddle attachment, mix the butter, sugar, coconut milk, and rum on low speed for 2 minutes. Add eggs one at a time and mix well after each addition. Scrape bowl. Add the sour cream and dry ingredients alternately, beginning with cream and ending with the flour.

Scoop the batter into the cupcake liners, filling them just below the rim. (I use a 2-ounce ice cream scoop.) Bake for 16 to 17 minutes or until a toothpick comes out clean.

2 *Prepare garnishes:* Place shredded coconut in a large skillet. Cook over medium heat, stirring frequently, until the flakes are evenly golden brown. Transfer to a plate to cool completely. Remove cherries from juice and let drain on a paper towel.

3 *Caramelize pineapple:* Melt butter, brown sugar, and vanilla in a saucepan over medium heat. Add half of the pineapple rings and cook for 2 minutes in a low boil. Flip over the rings and cook for 1 minute more. Transfer to plate to cool. Cook remaining pineapple with same method.

4 *Make the frosting:* Sift the powdered sugar and set aside.

In a mixer fitted with the paddle attachment, beat the cream cheese, butter, and vanilla on medium speed until blended. Scrape down the sides of the bowl well and mix for another 2 minutes to ensure no lumps remain.

Add the powdered sugar all at once and beat on low speed just until sugar is incorporated. Then beat at high speed for 10 seconds. Scrape down sides well. Beat the mixture again on high speed for 10 seconds.

5 Frost the cupcakes with the cream cheese frosting, crumb the edges with the toasted coconut, and top with a caramelized baby pineapple and maraschino cherry.

Cupcakes
- 1½ cups cake flour
- ¼ teaspoon baking powder
- ¼ teaspoon baking soda
- ¼ teaspoon salt
- ½ cup (1 stick) unsalted butter, room temperature
- 1¼ cups sugar
- ½ cup coconut milk
- ¼ cup Ron del Barrilito rum
- 2 large eggs
- ¼ cup sour cream
- 2 cups shredded sweetened coconut for garnish
- 14 maraschino cherries with stems for garnish

Caramelized Pineapple
- ½ cup (1 stick) unsalted butter
- ¾ cup light brown sugar
- 1 teaspoon pure vanilla extract
- 1 (28-ounce) can baby pineapple rings (I use Brover brand)

Cream Cheese Frosting
- 2 cups powdered sugar
- 6 ounces cream cheese, cold
- 5 tablespoons unsalted butter, at room temperature
- ½ teaspoon pure vanilla extract

If you have trouble finding baby pineapples, crushed pineapple is a fine substitute.

cookies and brownies

These days, the cookie seems to be the underdog. While specialty cookie shops are few and far between, everywhere you turn a new cupcake bakery opens. Many people believe it's because the cupcake is both nostalgic and visually appealing. While a cupcake may beat out the cookie in those areas, the cookie triumphs when it comes to versatility of textures, shapes, and sizes. They are easily transportable and can be eaten on the run or leisurely enjoyed crumbled over a scoop of ice cream. Warm or cold, sweet or savory, cookies remain delicious. And let's not forget the most popular sweet treat in the country: no, not a cupcake—it's the classic chocolate chip cookie developed by Ruth Graves Wakefield in the 1930s.

Many a beach experience would be incomplete without cookies, be it on a long coastal road trip or a quick sunbathing excursion. No matter how enjoyable the experience is, at some point, the need for something sweet and delicious calls. A cookie is the perfect treat to satisfy this craving. It's portable and can be enjoyed in just a few bites.

This is the largest chapter of the book for good reason. Mainly, I love cookies. I love creating them, making them, baking them, writing about them, and eating them. I did my best to include a wide variety of types of cookies, everything from rolled cookies and sandwich cookies to drop cookies and bars.

cocoa islands ★

Makes about 13 cookies

Cocoa Island is a small, private island resort in the Maldives designed for those seeking a relaxed getaway experience. Comprised of thirty-three romantic over-water suites and villas, this mini-heaven on Earth boasts some of the world's best beaches, snorkeling, and diving. Like the actual Cocoa Island, this cookie has an understated elegance combining smooth luscious salted caramel, crunchy sweet pecans, and decadent chewy chocolate.

Cookie dough

½ cup (1 stick) unsalted butter, at room temperature

¾ cup sugar

2 large eggs, separated

1 cup all-purpose flour

⅓ cup unsweetened cocoa powder

¼ teaspoon salt

⅛ cup whole milk

Garnish

1 cup pecans, finely chopped

Sea salt for sprinkling

Caramel Sauce

1½ cups sugar

½ cup water

¼ teaspoon lemon juice

1 cup heavy cream

¼ teaspoon salt

I prefer to use Maldon sea salt on these cookies. This salt can be found at specialty food stores.

1 Line a cookie tray with parchment paper or aluminum foil. Set aside.

2 In a mixer fitted with the paddle attachment, cream the butter and sugar on medium speed until light and fluffy, about one minute. Add in yolks and mix until combined. Beat in the flour, cocoa powder, and salt, followed by the milk.

3 Scoop the dough onto the prepared tray (I use a 1-ounce ice cream scoop), about 1-inch apart. Flatten each cookie with your palm to about 2 inches in diameter and ½ inches tall. Place cookie tray in refrigerator for 15 minutes to firm up dough.

4 *Prepare the garnishes:* In the meantime, preheat oven to 350 degrees. Whisk the egg whites in a small bowl to break them up. In another bowl, place the finely chopped pecans.

5 *Make the caramel sauce:* Stir together the sugar, water, and lemon juice in a heavy-bottomed medium saucepan. Heat the sugar over medium heat until the sugar is dissolved. If necessary, brush the insides of the pan with a wet pastry brush to wash down any crystals sticking to the sides.

Increase to high heat and bring to a boil, without stirring, until the sugar reaches a deep amber color, about 7 to 9 minutes.

Remove from heat and carefully whisk in the heavy cream. Be careful, as the caramel will sputter when you add the cream. If necessary, return to low heat to melt any clumps of caramel. Stir in the salt. Transfer the caramel to a dish, place in the refrigerator and let cool uncovered.

6 Gently remove the portioned cookies from tray and coat the edges of the cookie in the whisked egg whites. Then roll the edges in the pecans and place back on tray.

7 Bake for 12 to 13 minutes or until tops have puffed slightly. Remove from oven. Using the handle of an ice cream scoop (your thumb or a pestle also work well), make a ¼-inch deep indentation in the center of each cookie.

8 Once cookies are completely cool, pour caramel into the centers. A squeeze bottle for the caramel works well. Sprinkle a little or a lot of sea salt over caramel.

coco hut macaroons 9 ☀

Makes about 15 macaroons

Lining picturesque Palolem Beach in Goa, India, are rows of bungalows known as Coco Huts. Named after the dense forest of coconut palms that tower around them, these huts are popular lodging options for both international and domestic visitors to one of Western India's most beautiful beaches. From these huts, visitors can relax and soak up the warm rays of the sun from dusk to dawn.

3 cups shredded sweetened coconut

¾ cup sugar

4 large egg whites

1 teaspoon pure vanilla extract

1 Mix first three ingredients in a saucepan and stir constantly with a rubber spatula over medium heat until mixture thickens and dries up considerably, about 4 minutes or 165 degrees.

2 Transfer mixture to a medium bowl, and stir in the vanilla extract.

3 Let cool uncovered in the refrigerator. Stir occasionally to speed up the cooling process. Mixture must be completely cool before baking.

4 Preheat the oven to 325 degrees. Line a baking tray with parchment paper and grease lightly with pan spray.

5 Using a small ice cream scoop (I use a 1-ounce scoop), drop the batter in mounds 1-inch apart on the prepared baking tray. Bake for 10 minutes, rotate the tray, and then bake for an additional 10 minutes. Turn broiler on low and cook for 4 to 5 minutes. Rotate as necessary for even browning.

6 Remove from oven and let cool completely on tray. Store macaroons in the refrigerator in an airtight container.

For a delicious upgrade, dip the bottoms of the cooled macaroons in melted dark chocolate. Refrigerate on a parchment-lined cookie sheet until set up, about 20 minutes.

boardwalk butter cookies ★

Makes about 24 cookies

1 cup (2 sticks) unsalted butter, at room temperature

⅔ cup sugar

1 large egg

2 teaspoons pure vanilla extract

2½ cups all-purpose flour

½ teaspoon baking powder

2 cups dark chocolate, chopped

1 cup assorted confetti for garnish

Boardwalks are a staple of many major beaches along the East Coast and a stroll down any boardwalk is incomplete without a sweet confection. All along New Jersey's Atlantic City Boardwalk, the most famous of all beach promenades on the East Coast, vendors of popcorn, taffy, and ice cream abound. We are all aware of the natural disaster that shut down much of the Boardwalk in 2012 and the subsequent setbacks that followed. This cookie is my sweet ode to the communities that were affected and their perseverance.

1 Preheat the oven to 350 degrees. Line two cookie trays with parchment paper.

2 In a mixer fitted with the paddle attachment, mix the butter and sugar on medium speed until light and fluffy. Add the egg and vanilla extract and mix until combined. Add the flour and baking powder and mix for 1 minute until thoroughly combined.

3 Transfer the cookie dough to a piping bag fitted with the large ribbon tube. Pipe the batter into 2-inch long strips.

4 Bake for 8 to 10 minutes or until golden brown on the edges.

5 Melt the chocolate in the microwave, stirring every 30 seconds. When the cookies have cooled completely, dip them in the melted chocolate and sprinkle with confetti. Place on a parchment-lined tray to allow chocolate to set up completely.

Try sandwiching two of these cookies with raspberry jam to make a doubly extra good cookie!

andes mint biscotti ☼

Makes about 25 biscotti

The colors of Miami and South Beach are something special. Nowhere else in the world where ocean meets land does every color pop and sizzle as they do around the beaches of South Florida. Whether it's the beautiful orange hue of a rising sun over Key West or the neon flash after midnight on South Beach, the colors define a unique experience.

With a cookie like biscotti it's important to feature some distinguishing flavor or color to make it memorable beyond a dry and crispy cookie usually needing to be dunked in a beverage. In this cookie, the strikingly beautiful sea green color catches the eye first, followed by the surprising pop of Andes mint that gives excitement to an otherwise standard cookie eating experience.

1 box (28 pieces) Andes mints

2¼ cups all-purpose flour

1 teaspoon baking soda

3 large eggs

¾ cup sugar

1 teaspoon pure vanilla extract

1 drop green food color

Pinch of salt

1 Preheat the oven to 300 degrees. Grease a cookie sheet with pan spray and line with parchment paper.

2 Unwrap all the mints and cut them into small pieces. I like to cut each mint into 8 small squares. Set aside.

3 Sift the flour and baking soda. Set aside.

4 In a mixer fitted with the whip attachment, combine the eggs, sugar, vanilla, food color, and salt. Whip until light and thick, about 3 to 4 minutes.

5 Add the dry ingredients to the egg mixture and mix just until incorporated. Fold in the mint pieces with a rubber spatula. Dough will be thick and sticky.

6 Transfer the dough to the prepared tray, shaping it as a log the length of the cookie sheet. Using flour as needed, shape and flatten the dough to about 13 inches long and 3 inches wide. Finished dough should be about a ½ inch thick.

7 Bake for 35 to 40 minutes, or when the cookie is firm to the touch and just slightly browned. Remove from the oven, and let cool for 5 minutes. Decrease the oven temperature to 275 degrees.

8 Transfer the warm cookie to a cutting board. Using a serrated knife, cut ½-inch slices at a diagonal. Lay the sliced cookies cut-side down back onto the sheet tray and bake in the oven for 10 minutes. Remove from oven, flip each cookie over and bake for 10 minutes more.

9 Let cool completely before serving. Store in an airtight container at room temperature.

Biscotti keep well in the freezer. Simply wrap them in foil and freeze them in resealable plastic bags for up to 3 weeks.

modern snickerdoodle

Makes about 13 cookies

Cookies

½ cup (1 stick) unsalted
butter, at room
temperature

½ cup sugar

1 large egg

1¼ cups all-purpose flour

1½ teaspoons baking
powder

½ teaspoon ground
Indonesian cinnamon

¼ teaspoon salt

Cinnamon sugar

1 cup sugar

1 teaspoon ground
Indonesian cinnamon

*At Sugar Blossom, we make
these gluten free by substituting the flour with Namaste
Perfect Flour Blend, which
can be found at most natural
food stores.*

One of the most incredible beach getaways has to be to the island of Bali. While there, a can't miss experience is an authentic Bali beachside cinnamon scrub. The intoxicating aroma of cinnamon surrounding you during this spa treatment is perfectly captured by my Modern Snickerdoodle. To enhance and update my Snickerdoodle's sweet cinnamon flavor, I blend cinnamon into the cookie dough *before* baking. As the warm, just baked cookies get tossed in copious amounts of Indonesian cinnamon and sugar, the sounds of the waves lapping at the beach will drown out any other thoughts of this being just an ordinary day.

1 Preheat the oven to 350 degrees. Line a cookie sheet with aluminum foil or parchment paper. Set aside.

2 In a mixer fitted with the paddle attachment, cream the butter and sugar on medium speed until smooth, about 1 minute. Add egg and mix until incorporated. Scrape bowl. Add the flour, baking powder, cinnamon, and salt. Mix until combined.

3 Scoop the dough onto the prepared trays (I use a 1-ounce ice cream scoop), and bake for 12 to 14 minutes, or until the cookies feel firm when pressed gently on top. Remove from oven and let the cookies cool for 10 minutes on the cookie sheet.

4 Combine the sugar and cinnamon in a bowl. Toss the warm cookies in the mixture. Let cool completely on a wire rack.

panko cookies

Makes approximately 9 cookies

I love textures in my cookies, everything from crunchy to chewy to fleshy. When I bake, I enjoy experimenting with dried and fresh fruit, nuts, chips, cereal, and candy, adding them to my cookies every chance I get to make them more interesting. The unique ingredient in these cookies always helps to get a conversation started at my beach parties. While Panko is normally seen in savory dishes, it is a welcome presence in this sweet butter cookie, adding a nice, crunchy texture that does indeed remain crunchy for days.

1 Preheat the oven to 350 degrees. Line a cookie tray with aluminum foil or parchment paper.

2 In a mixer fitted with a paddle attachment, cream the butter, powdered sugar, and vanilla on medium speed until light and fluffy, about 2 minutes. Add the flour and panko, and beat on low speed until blended.

3 Scoop the dough onto the prepared tray (I use a 1-ounce ice cream scoop). Press down slightly on the dough to flatten it to about ½ inches tall. Bake for 7 minutes, rotate, and then bake 7 to 8 minutes more or until bottoms of cookies are lightly browned.

4 Cool 10 minutes on baking sheet. Roll warm cookies in the powdered sugar until evenly coated. Place on a wire rack to cool completely before tossing again in the powdered sugar. Store in an airtight container at room temperature.

½ cup (1 stick) unsalted butter, at room temperature

¼ cup powdered sugar, sifted

1 teaspoon pure vanilla extract

1 cup all-purpose flour

½ cup panko bread crumbs

About 2 cups of sifted powdered sugar for coating

old-fashioned peanut butter cookies ☼

Makes about 23 cookies

½ cup (1 stick) unsalted butter, at room temperature

½ cup smooth peanut butter

½ cup light brown sugar

½ cup sugar

1 large egg

1 tablespoon half-and-half

1 teaspoon pure vanilla extract

1½ cups all-purpose flour

Heaping ½ cup peanut butter chips

¾ teaspoon baking soda

¼ teaspoon salt

Growing up on the East Coast, I would often head to Virginia Beach during spring break. This popular tourist destination boasts miles of sandy beaches as well as amazing fishing and boating opportunities. It's also famous for its peanut specialties, including peanut brittle, peanut pie, and fried peanuts. When I hit the beaches these days, I love packing these soft and chewy cookies in my beach bag. The heat of the sun warms the cookie just enough to bring out the aroma of the peanut butter and melts the peanut butter chips embedded in the dough. It's like taking a bite out of a just-baked peanut butter cookie that's melt-in-your-mouth delicious, all while being at the beach.

1 In a mixer fitted with the paddle attachment, cream the butter, peanut butter, and sugars on medium speed until light and fluffy, about 2 minutes. Add the egg, half-and-half, and vanilla extract, and mix for an additional minute. Mix in the flour, chips, baking soda, and salt until incorporated. Cover the bowl and place in the refrigerator for 1 hour.

2 Preheat oven to 375 degrees. Line a couple baking trays with aluminum foil or parchment paper.

3 Scoop the dough onto the prepared trays (I use a 1-ounce ice cream scoop). Flatten slightly with palm. Mark the dough with the back of a fork in a crisscross pattern.

4 Bake for 9 to 10 minutes, or until edges are just set. Cookies will look underbaked. Remove from oven and let the cookies cool completely on the sheet trays.

sweet and salty beach bod brittle 9 ★ ⏰

Makes about 2 cups

1 cup sugar

½ cup light corn syrup

¼ cup water

½ teaspoon + ¼ teaspoon salt, separated

2 tablespoons unsalted butter, at room temperature

1 teaspoon baking soda

1½ cups salted, roasted whole cashews

The cashew is a beautiful nut. (Yes, I know it's botanically a legume, but nobody ever uses that word.) Its smooth skin, golden tan, and curvaceous shape—all the traits of the ultimate beach bod—seem to make it the most physically blessed of all nuts. Take a trip to Brazil, one of the top producers of the cashew, and you'll be overwhelmed with these sights as well. I'm talking about the tranquil and remote cashew-shaped beaches of San Miguel and Praia do Riacho in the northeast Brazilian state Algagoas. Off the beaten path, it's worth the drive on the local coastal road through rural beach villages to get there. Stay in the beach town of Praia do Toque and from there explore the undisturbed beauty of Brazil's most remote beaches.

1 Coat a clean, flat cookie sheet with pan spray and set aside.

2 In a heavy 2-quart saucepan, bring to a boil the sugar, corn syrup, water, and ½ teaspoon salt over medium heat. Continue cooking until the sugar mixture reaches a nice light amber color. If needed, swirl the pan for even coloring.

3 Remove from the heat. Carefully whisk in the butter followed by the baking soda. The mixture will rise and bubble. Quickly stir in the nuts with a rubber spatula, then immediately pour the brittle onto the prepared cookie sheet. Use the back of a greased spoon or spatula to spread the brittle out. Use two forks to pull and stretch the edges of the brittle to thin out larger clumps of brittle. Sprinkle ¼ teaspoon salt over the brittle.

4 Let the brittle cool completely, and then snap into pieces. The brittle can be stored at room temperature, in an airtight container, for up to two weeks.

This brittle is excellent crushed and served over ice cream.

crannie macs

Makes about 24 cookies

Loaded with cranberries, this cookie will have you dreaming of a low-key beach escape to the cranberry haven of Cape Cod, Massachusetts. With more than 500 miles of unspoiled coastline, Cape Cod offers beaches of different types, from full-amenity beaches with warm gentle waves to roaring surf along desolate stretches of sand. While there, drop by a local cranberry farm. Southeastern Massachusetts is home to more than 14,000 acres of working cranberry bogs.

1 Preheat the oven to 350 degrees. Line a baking sheet with aluminum foil or parchment paper. Set aside.

2 In a mixer fitted with the paddle attachment, cream the butter and sugars on medium speed for 2 minutes until light and fluffy. Add the egg and vanilla, and mix for 1 minute. Scrape bowl well.

Add the flour, white chocolate chips, nuts, cranberries, baking soda, and salt. Mix on low speed until incorporated.

3 Scoop the dough onto the prepared trays (I use a 1-ounce ice cream scoop). Bake for 12 to 14 minutes, or until lightly browned. Remove from oven and let the cookies cool completely on the sheet trays.

⅓ cup unsalted butter, at room temperature

½ cup light brown sugar

¼ cup sugar

1 large egg

1½ teaspoons pure vanilla extract

1 cup all-purpose flour

1 cup white chocolate chips

1 cup macadamia nuts, coarsely chopped

1 cup dried cranberries

¼ teaspoon baking soda

¼ teaspoon salt

flat and chewy chocolate chip cookies

Makes approximately 31 cookies

I worked long and hard to develop a recipe that would satisfy my brother's request for a chocolate chip cookie that was flat, crispy on the edges and chewy in the center. Finally after many attempts, I received his sweet sound of approval: *mmmmm.* Besides its incredible flavors of caramelized sugar and sweet butter, this cookie is loaded with mini chocolate chips to ensure that each bite hits you like a wave of chocolate.

1⅔ cups all-purpose flour

¾ teaspoon baking soda

½ teaspoon salt

1 (12-ounce) package semi-sweet mini chocolate chips

1 cup (2 sticks) unsalted butter, at room temperature

1 cup light brown sugar

⅔ cup + 3 tablespoons sugar

2 large eggs

1 Preheat the oven to 375 degrees. Line a few sheet pans with parchment paper or aluminum foil.

2 Combine the flour, baking soda, salt, and chocolate chips in a bowl. Set aside.

3 In a mixer fitted with the paddle attachment, cream the butter and sugars on medium speed until light and fluffy, about 1 minute. Add eggs one at a time, scraping well after each addition. Add the dry ingredients, and mix until incorporated.

4 Scoop the dough onto the prepared sheet pans (I use a 1-ounce ice cream scoop), and bake for 10 to 12 minutes, or until the cookies are lightly browned all over.

5 Remove from oven and let the cookies cool on the sheet pans.

These cookies are best eaten the day they're made. You can store extra dough in the refrigerator and bake when desired so you can eat them fresh every time.

gluten-free chocolate chip cookies 9

Makes about 16 cookies

½ cup + 3 tablespoons white rice flour

¼ cup potato flour

2 tablespoons tapioca flour

⅓ teaspoon xanthan gum

¼ teaspoon baking soda

¼ teaspoon salt

1 cup semi-sweet chocolate chips

6 tablespoons (¾ stick) unsalted butter, at room temperature

½ cup dark brown sugar

¼ cup sugar

1 large egg

1 teaspoon pure vanilla extract

It has become clear that *gluten free* is a strong and growing trend in the food industry. The good news is that gluten-free flours and ingredients have continued to improve from the early days when there was a definite difference in taste from traditional flour products. I'm including gluten-free desserts in this book that taste as delicious as my other recipes even if you are not gluten sensitive.

1 Preheat the oven to 350 degrees. Line a couple cookie trays with parchment paper or aluminum foil.

2 Whisk all dry ingredients together in a bowl. Add chocolate chips to mixture and set aside.

3 In a mixer fitted with the paddle attachment, cream butter and sugars on medium speed until light and fluffy, about 2 minutes. Scrape bowl. Add egg and vanilla and mix until incorporated. Scrape bowl. Add dry ingredients and mix for 1 minute on low speed.

4 Scoop the dough onto the prepared trays (I use a 1-ounce ice cream scoop), and bake for 13 to 14 minutes or until just lightly browned on edges. Remove from oven and let cool completely on trays.

coconut apricot oat crisps ★

Makes approximately 30 cookies

Warning: these cookies are habit-forming. They are thin, buttery, sweet, crispy cookies that are impossible to resist. The bits of dried apricot in these cookies always remind me of bright afternoons at the beach. One of my favorite sunny beach memories is from the east coast of Mexico. Here amongst the tourist-laden Caribbean beaches, one can escape to the secluded beach of Tulum. You can swim away your cares with the backdrop of *El Castillo*, the old Mayan temple that is the centerpiece of Tulum.

1 Preheat the oven to 375 degrees. Line a few sheet pans with parchment paper or aluminum foil. Set aside.

2 In a mixer fitted with the paddle attachment, mix the butter and sugars on medium speed until light and fluffy, about 2 minutes. Add egg and vanilla extract and mix until combined. Add the flour, apricots, coconut, oats, baking soda, and salt. Mix until incorporated.

3 Scoop the dough onto the prepared trays (I use a 1-ounce ice cream scoop), and bake for 10 minutes. Gently bang the sheet pans on the rack and rotate. Bake for an additional 1 to 2 minutes until the center of cookie is barely white.

4 Remove from oven and let the cookies cool on the sheet pans.

1 cup (2 sticks) unsalted butter, at room temperature

1 cup sugar

½ cup light brown sugar

1 large egg

1 teaspoon pure vanilla extract

1⅓ cups all-purpose flour

1 cup dried apricots, diced

1 cup shredded sweetened coconut

½ cup rolled oats

1 teaspoon baking soda

½ teaspoon salt

tsunamis

Makes about 40 cookies

1 cup (2 sticks) unsalted butter, at room temperature

¾ cup sugar

¾ cup light brown sugar

1 large egg

1 teaspoon pure vanilla extract

1½ cups all-purpose flour

1½ cups rolled oats

1 cup dried cherries

1 cup chocolate chips

1 cup toffee bits (about 4 chopped SKOR bars)

1 teaspoon baking soda

I call this cookie Tsunami because it is jam-packed with buttery toffee, chocolate, and tart cherries. With one bite of this cookie, you will ride a tidal wave all the way to Shirahama Beach in Japan. Aside from its gorgeous white sand beach, Shirahama offers a "tsunami" of sights, including hot springs, open air baths, the unusual rock formations of Senjojiki Coast, and an undersea observation tower. I recommend visiting during the summer months, as you will be treated to incredible fireworks each night.

1 Preheat the oven to 350 degrees. Line a few sheet pans with parchment paper or aluminum foil.

2 In a mixer fitted with the paddle attachment, mix the butter and sugars on medium speed until light and fluffy, about 2 minutes. Add egg and vanilla extract and mix until combined. Add the flour, oats, cherries, chocolate, toffee bits, and baking soda. Mix until incorporated. Dough will be somewhat stiff.

3 Scoop the dough onto the prepared trays (I use a 1-ounce ice cream scoop), and press down the tops of the dough slightly. Bake for 10 to 11 minutes, until golden brown all over. Remove from oven and let the cookies cool on the sheet pans.

bulleit bourbon fudge brownies ★

Makes one 10-inch square pan

Brownies

1½ cups (3 sticks) unsalted butter, at room temperature

12 ounces dark chocolate, chopped

6 large eggs

3½ cups sugar

1 cup unsweetened cocoa powder

¾ cup cake flour, sifted

2 tablespoons Bulleit bourbon whiskey (or your preferred whiskey)

Whiskey glaze

1 cup powdered sugar, sifted

2 tablespoons unsweetened cocoa powder

2 tablespoons Bulleit bourbon whiskey (or your preferred whiskey)

2 tablespoons hot water 1 teaspoon pure vanilla extract

To make these kid-friendly, simply skip the glaze and omit the alcohol from the brownie batter.

Chocolate is transporting. The finest makes you feel like you are diving into a pool of warm, silky-smooth luxury with every bite. Where better to envision this pool than the stunning country of France. On the Mediterranean coast, you will find Marseille, the second largest city after Paris. To escape the crowds, take a boat to the carefully preserved and uninhabited beach of L'Ile de Riou. Named the best diving spot in France, L'Ile de Riou is a popular destination for scuba diving, snorkeling, and swimming. So put on your baking gear and dive into this luxurious pool of chocolate. These brownies are so fudgy and decadent, you won't want to come up for air. For an even bigger indulgence, warm a slice of this brownie in the microwave for 30 seconds, top with ice cream, and treat yourself to the most amazing brownie sundae ever.

1 Preheat the oven to 325 degrees. Grease a 10-inch square baking pan and line the bottom with parchment paper.

2 Melt the butter and chocolate together in a medium bowl set over simmering water. Allow to cool for 10 minutes. Meanwhile, in the bowl of an electric mixer fitted with the paddle attachment, mix the eggs and sugar for 1 minute. Blend in the cocoa powder. Pour in the chocolate mixture and mix well. Add flour to the chocolate mixture and mix just until incorporated. Fold in the whiskey with a rubber spatula. Spread evenly in the prepared pan. Bake for 1 hour.

3 While brownie is baking, prepare glaze. Whisk together all the ingredients in a medium bowl. Set aside.

4 Remove brownie from oven and pour whiskey glaze over the top of the warm brownie. Tilt pan to spread glaze. Return the pan to the oven, and bake for an additional 2 minutes. Remove from the oven and cool on counter for 30 minutes. Transfer to refrigerator to cool completely. Cut into bars and store in an airtight container at room temperature or in refrigerator.

sugar layouts ☼

Makes 1½ pounds cookie dough

Among Maui's scores of beaches, Little Beach stands out as a favorite of those wishing to get the perfect tan. Sunbathers flock to this one-eighth-mile long beach for its low-key ambiance and turquoise waters. Here you can lay out au natural and focus on evening out your tan. Stay late on a Sunday and enjoy the weekly local ritual of fire dancing. Clothing optional, sugar cookies recommended.

1 Preheat oven to 350 degrees. Line sheet trays with parchment paper or aluminum foil.

2 In a mixer fitted with the paddle attachment, cream the butter and sugar on medium speed until light and fluffy, about 2 minutes. Beat in the egg, milk, and extracts. Scrape bowl. Add the flour and baking powder and mix until incorporated. Wrap dough with plastic and chill in refrigerator for at least 1 hour.

3 Roll out dough on floured surface to ¼-inch thickness. Cut into desired shapes and bake approximately 10 minutes or until edges are slightly browned. Baking time will depend on shape of cookie; bake longer for a crispier cookie. Remove from oven and let cool completely on tray before decorating.

4 *Make the icing:* Combine the powdered sugar and meringue powder in a mixer fitted with the whip attachment. With the mixer on low speed, slowly drizzle in the cold water. Beat on medium speed for 1 minute. Add more water if needed. Use immediately.

Cookies

½ cup (1 stick) unsalted butter, at room temperature

½ cup sugar

1 large egg

2 tablespoons whole milk

1 teaspoon pure vanilla extract

½ teaspoon pure almond extract

2 cups all-purpose flour

¾ teaspoon baking powder

Royal Icing

1 pound powdered sugar, sifted

3 tablespoons meringue powder

6 tablespoons cold water

This dough is perfect for making cookie pops. Simply roll the cookie dough to ½-inch thickness, cut into desired shape, and slide lollipop sticks into dough. Slide the stick in straight and at least 1½ inches deep. Place a flat strip of dough on the back of the cookie directly behind the lollipop stick. Bake as usual.

the ultimate road trip cookie ♥v☼

Makes approximately 14 cookies

½ cup margarine, at room temperature

½ cup sugar

⅓ cup light brown sugar

2 teaspoons pure vanilla extract

¼ cup soy milk

1 cup all-purpose flour

1 cup rolled oats

½ cup dried cranberries

½ cup dairy-free chocolate chips

½ teaspoon ground cinnamon

¼ teaspoon baking soda

¼ teaspoon baking powder

This soft vegan cookie is my go-to treat to bring on coastal road trips. I can always count on these cookies to stay tasty over the course of the trip, while also providing much-needed nourishment. I know I'm biased, but the prettiest coastal road trip in my mind is California's iconic Highway 1. This cliff-hugging route winds more than 500 miles in California, most of it along the state's coastline. From Monterey to Big Sur to Santa Barbara, these sweet delights will keep you smiling all the way.

1 Preheat oven to 350 degrees. Line a cookie tray with aluminum foil.

2 In a mixer fitted with the paddle attachment, cream the margarine, sugars, and vanilla on medium speed for 1 minute. Mix in the soy milk. Add the flour, oats, cranberries, chocolate chips, cinnamon, baking soda, and baking powder. Mix on low speed until all ingredients are incorporated.

3 Scoop the dough onto the prepared cookie tray. (I use a 1-ounce ice cream scoop.) Bake for 8 minutes, rotate, then bake for an additional 5 to 7 minutes or until top of cookies are set.

4 Remove from oven and let the cookies cool completely on the cookie tray.

molasses cookies

Makes about 20 cookies

½ cup (1 stick) unsalted butter, at room temperature

1 cup dark brown sugar

¼ cup molasses

1 large egg

2 cups all-purpose flour

1 tablespoon ground ginger

1 teaspoon baking soda

½ teaspoon ground cinnamon

Pinch of ground cloves

2 cups turbinado sugar for rolling

It seems like a good bet that you probably won't find a jar of molasses in your cupboard right now. This thick syrup is usually made from boiling the juice of sugar cane or sugar beets. The result is a dark and delicious ingredient that might be worth adding to your shopping list the next time you go to your local beach market. Molasses seems to make an appearance around the holidays, but this soft and chewy cookie is perfect any time of the year.

1 Preheat oven to 350 degrees. Line a couple cookie trays with aluminum foil or parchment paper.

2 In a mixer fitted with the paddle attachment, cream butter and sugar on medium speed for 1 minute. Drizzle in molasses and beat mixture until light and fluffy, about 2 minutes. Add egg and mix until incorporated. Scrape bowl. Mix in flour, ginger, baking soda, cinnamon, and cloves on low speed until combined.

3 Pour the turbinado sugar in a small bowl. Using a 1-ounce ice cream scoop, portion the dough and drop it into the bowl of sugar. Roll in the sugar and place on cookie tray. Flatten cookie slightly with your palm.

4 Bake for 12 to 13 minutes until cracks appear on top and edges are just lightly browned. Remove from oven and let the cookies cool completely on the cookie tray.

ginger bay cabana boys ☼

Makes about 13 cookies

Off the Southeast coast of Barbados lays a secluded beach known as Ginger Bay. It's the perfect setting for couples looking for a romantic escape. The beach gets few visitors so explore hidden caves at your leisure and expect to be surrounded only by swaying palms. Make sure to pack a lunch including some of these Cabana Boys, as there are no amenities or services provided.

1 Preheat oven to 350 degrees. Line several cookie trays with parchment paper.

2 In a mixer fitted with the paddle attachment, cream butter and sugar on medium speed until light and fluffy, about 2 minutes. Beat in molasses and egg yolk for 1 minute. Add flour, salt, baking powder, baking soda, and spices and mix until combined. Wrap dough and chill for at least 1 hour in refrigerator.

3 On a lightly floured surface, roll the dough out to ¼-inch thickness. Cut into desired shapes with cookie cutters. Place cookies at least 1 inch apart on prepared trays.

4 Bake 8 to 10 minutes, or until cookies puff and edges are lightly browned. Remove from oven and let cookies completely on tray. Frost with Royal Icing when cool.

5 *Make the icing:* Combine the powdered sugar and meringue powder in a mixer fitted with the whip attachment. With the mixer on low speed, slowly drizzle in the cold water. Beat on medium speed for 2 minutes. Add more water if needed. Use immediately.

½ cup (1 stick) unsalted butter, at room temperature

½ cup sugar

½ cup molasses

1 large egg yolk

2 cups all-purpose flour

½ teaspoon salt

½ teaspoon baking powder

½ teaspoon baking soda

1 teaspoon ground ginger

1 teaspoon ground cloves

½ teaspoon ground nutmeg

Royal Icing

1 pound powdered sugar, sifted

3 tablespoons meringue powder

6 tablespoons cold water

pumpkin beach ball whoopee pies

Makes about 20 whoopee pies

Cookies

1½ cups all-purpose flour

1 teaspoon baking soda

½ teaspoon baking powder

¼ teaspoon ground cinnamon

¼ teaspoon ground ginger

¼ teaspoon ground nutmeg

¼ teaspoon salt

6 tablespoons (¾ stick) unsalted butter, at room temperature

1 cup light brown sugar

¾ cup canned pure pumpkin

1 large egg

¼ cup half-and-half

1 teaspoon pure vanilla extract

Mousse

1 cup heavy cream, chilled

6 tablespoons sugar

8 ounces cream cheese, softened

1 teaspoon pure vanilla extract

Powdered sugar, colored sprinkles for garnish

A day at the beach is incomplete without a beach ball. Its lightweight and soft squishy surface make it the perfect companion for summer fun. Most notably, its bands of bright colors prevent it from blending into the sand so you can keep an eye on it through the hazy heat. I love pumpkin cookies, but I always disliked how plain and boring they looked after baking. Even with the customary drizzle of glaze, they never looked appetizing to me. So I decided one day to make them into whoopee pies and coat the edges with colorful sprinkles. The colors jump out just like on a beach ball. Now that's more like it!

1 Preheat oven to 350 degrees. Line a couple sheet pans with parchment paper or aluminum foil.

2 Sift together the flour, baking soda, baking powder, cinnamon, ginger, nutmeg, and salt. Set aside.

3 In a mixer fitted with the paddle attachment, cream the butter and brown sugar on medium speed for 1 minute. Add pumpkin and continue mixing until combined. Add egg, half-and-half, and vanilla. Mix on medium speed for 2 minutes. Mix in the flour mixture on low speed until incorporated.

4 Scoop the dough onto the prepared cookie tray. (I use a 1-ounce ice cream scoop.) Press down dough slightly with palm. Bake for 9 to 10 minutes or until top of cookies are set. Remove from oven and set aside to cool.

5 *Make the mousse:* In a mixer fitted with the whisk attachment, whip the heavy cream and sugar to medium peaks. Transfer the whipped cream to a small clean bowl and set aside. Add the cream cheese and vanilla extract to the mixing bowl and using the paddle attachment, beat the cheese until smooth. Remove the bowl from the mixer and vigorously whisk in the whipped cream.

6 Transfer the mousse to a piping bag fitted with a medium smooth tip (I use a ½-inch diameter tip). Pipe a dollop of filling in the center of one cookie and sandwich with another, pressing down gently. Coat the edges of the pies with colored sprinkles and garnish with powdered sugar. (Tip: if filled pie is too unwieldy to coat with sprinkles, simply place them in the freezer for a few minutes to firm up slightly.)

santorini exalted ★

Makes one 9x13-inch pan or 24 servings

1 cup (2 sticks) unsalted butter, melted

1 pound walnuts, chopped

½ cup sugar

2 tablespoons ground cinnamon

1 (1-pound) box of phyllo dough, thawed

Syrup

1 cup water

1 cup sugar

½ cup orange blossom honey

1 lemon peel

1 cinnamon stick

I'm pretty much a purist when it comes to Baklava. I prefer to use solely walnuts (California grown, of course), cinnamon as the only spice, and a smaller than usual amount of sugar so the flavors of toasted nuts, honey, and cinnamon shine through. This likely stems from my love of the natural breathtaking scenery of the Greek island of Santorini. From whitewashed cliff-side villages, one can gaze out on endless views of the ocean in every direction. It really is picture perfect and unspoiled in every way.

1 Preheat oven to 350 degrees. Lightly butter the bottom and sides of a 9x13-inch pan with a pastry brush.

2 Combine the walnuts, sugar, and cinnamon in a medium bowl. Set aside.

3 Lay 1 phyllo layer down in the prepared pan and butter lightly. Repeat 10 times. Spread *half* of the nut mixture on top. Repeat with another 10 layers of phyllo dough, buttering each layer. Spread the remaining nut mixture on top. Layer 5 more layers of phyllo dough on top, buttering each one. Chill for 30 minutes in refrigerator.

4 Using a sharp knife, cut the baklava into desired shapes. I prefer to cut 2x2-inch squares and then cut them in half diagonally. Bake for 50 to 55 minutes until golden and crisp.

5 *Prepare the syrup*: Boil all ingredients in a small saucepan for 10 minutes over medium-high heat. Strain the syrup and then pour it over the top of the warm, just-baked baklava.

6 Let the baklava cool uncovered. Store at room temperature lightly covered. Do not refrigerate.

apricot pistachio rolls

Makes 12 large or 16 small rugelach

Roll down the Aegean coast of western Turkey, the world's leading apricot producer, and you will arrive in Cesme. This picturesque town is home to Turkish elite as well as international residents drawn to the area's thermal springs and crystal clear warm waters. Scores of luxury resorts line the beach and provide their guests with first-class care and attention. As you roll up the sweet apricot jam and crunchy pistachios in the soft cream cheese dough, imagine yourself basking in the bright orange hue of the sun and the warm breeze of Cesme.

1 Preheat the oven to 375 degrees. Line a sheet tray with aluminum foil or parchment paper.

2 *Make the dough:* In a mixer fitted with the paddle attachment, beat the cream cheese and butter on medium speed until light and fluffy, about 2 minutes. Make sure to scrape bowl occasionally to ensure mixture is smooth. Add flour, sugar, and salt. Mix until dough comes together. Shape dough into a disc and wrap in plastic wrap. Chill for 30 minutes in the refrigerator.

3 *Make the topping:* Measure out the milk and set aside. Combine the sugar and cinnamon in a small bowl and blend together.

4 *Make the filling:* On a floured surface, roll out the dough into a circle about 14 inches in diameter. Using a mini offset spatula, spread the apricot jam on the dough leaving a ½-inch rim. Sprinkle *half* the cinnamon mixture over the jam, followed by the pistachios.

5 Cut into 12 (or 16) equal wedges and tightly roll up each one starting at the wide end. Work the dough as gently as you can to maintain a nice height for the cookie. Place seam-side down onto the prepared sheet tray. Place the tray of rugelach in the refrigerator for 15 minutes. This will help the cookies maintain their shape when baked.

6 Brush tops of cookies with milk. Sprinkle remaining cinnamon sugar over tops of cookies. Bake for 10 minutes, rotate tray, then bake for 10 minutes more or until lightly brown on the edges.

7 Remove from oven and let the cookies cool completely on the sheet tray.

Dough

5 ounces cream cheese, softened

¾ cup (1½ sticks) unsalted butter, softened

1¼ cups all-purpose flour

1 tablespoon sugar

¼ teaspoon salt

Topping

¼ cup whole milk

5 teaspoons sugar

½ teaspoon ground cinnamon

Filling

7 teaspoons apricot jam

½ cup unsalted, dry roasted pistachios, finely chopped

paradise cookie pie ☀

Makes a 9-inch round cookie

1 cup sliced almonds

½ cup candied fruit mix

¼ cup all-purpose flour

¼ teaspoon salt

6 tablespoons (¾ stick) unsalted butter

⅔ cup sugar

⅓ cup whole milk

3 tablespoons clover honey

This is my beach house version of the classic European confection known as Florentine. While there is no concrete proof that this chewy, candy-like confection originated in Florence, the hopeless romantic in me believes it must. Where else would such a brilliant concoction of caramelized nuts and candied fruit come from but a land of such beauty, culture, and art? As you take in the piazzas, churches, and scores of museums, snack on these Florentines for that added energy boost. When you tire of navigating through the crowds, grab your beach bag and take a three-hour train ride to the Maremma region of Tuscany. The beaches of Maremma are among the best in Italy—clean, uncrowded, and blessed with cool waters and white sand.

1 Preheat the oven to 350 degrees. Coat a 9-inch round pan with nonstick spray, line the bottom with parchment paper cut to fit, then spray again.

2 In a stainless steel bowl, combine the almonds, candied fruit, flour, and salt. Set aside.

3 Place the butter, sugar, milk, and honey in a medium saucepan and cook over medium-high until mixture reaches 238 degrees. The mixture will boil with small bubbles all over the top and will have thickened considerably. Remove pot from the heat and stir in the fruit and nut mixture until well combined.

4 Pour the filling into the prepared cake pan and spread to the edges. Bake for 20 minutes or until the filling is bubbling and has turned light golden brown all over. Remove from oven and let cool completely at room temperature.

5 Run a paring knife along edge of cookie. Invert pan and pat bottom of pan to shake out cookie. Remove parchment and place the cookie on a cutting board. Cut into wedges. Store in an airtight container at room temperature.

madeleines ⏰

Makes about 18 cakes

These light sponge cakes make the perfect beach house–warming gift. Shaped like a perfect shell, I like to wrap them in clear cellophane bags and tie them with a colored ribbon before giving them away. I use lemon zest in my recipe, but you can omit or replace with the zest of other citrus fruits.

1 Preheat the oven to 350 degrees. Grease the Madeleine molds with pan spray. Gently sift flour evenly over the molds.

2 In the bowl of an electric mixer fitted with the whip attachment, beat the eggs, sugar, lemon zest, and vanilla on high speed for 3 minutes until thickened and yellow. Add the flour and baking powder and mix on low speed until combined. Remove bowl from

mixer and fold in the melted butter with a rubber spatula.

3 Fill each mold with the batter (I like to use a small ice cream scoop). Use a mini offset spatula to spread the batter out.

4 Bake for 8 to 10 minutes or until tops are set. Do not over bake.

¼ cup all-purpose flour for coating pan

3 large eggs

½ cup sugar

1 teaspoon finely grated lemon zest

½ teaspoon pure vanilla extract

¾ cup cake flour, sifted

¾ teaspoon baking powder

6 tablespoons (¾ stick) unsalted butter, melted and cooled slightly

reese's pieces chocolate drops ⏰

Makes about 24 drops

1 (12-ounce) package semi-sweet chocolate chips

¼ cup (½ stick) unsalted butter

1 (14-ounce) can condensed milk

½ teaspoon pure vanilla extract

1 cup all-purpose flour

1 teaspoon baking powder

¼ teaspoon salt

½ cup Reese's pieces candies

These irresistible cookies are chewy and rich with chocolate. Making them even better, each bite is highlighted with a wave of peanut butter and candy crunch. Don't hesitate to make the full batch of these cookies as they are even better the next day.

1 Preheat oven to 350 degrees. Line two cookie sheets with aluminum foil or parchment paper.

2 Melt chocolate chips and butter in a medium saucepan over low heat.

3 Remove from heat and transfer chocolate mixture to a mixer fitted with a paddle attachment. Add the condensed milk and vanilla extract. Mix on low speed until incorporated.

4 Mix in the flour, baking powder, and salt on low speed for 30 seconds. Remove bowl from mixer. Gently fold in the candy with a rubber spatula and mix just until combined.

5 Scoop the dough onto the prepared trays (I use a 1-ounce scoop) and bake for 12 to 13 minutes, rotating once halfway. Let cool on the sheet pans for at least 10 minutes before serving.

beach blondies ★☀

Makes one 8-inch square pan

Blondes are so overrated. Wait, did I just say that? I meant Blondies. For years I didn't get what was so great about blondies. They were always so overwhelmingly sweet. Then I tinkered with the recipe and figured out how to make these treats more appealing and tasty. The trick is to brown the butter, use dark brown sugar, and toast the walnuts beforehand. All of these steps ensure the richest, most flavorful, and decadent treat that is downright irresistible.

½ cup chopped walnuts

½ cup (1 stick) unsalted butter

¾ cup dark brown sugar

¼ cup sugar

1 large egg

1 teaspoon pure vanilla extract

1 cup all-purpose flour

¼ teaspoon salt

½ cup semi-sweet chocolate chunks

1 (1.4-ounce) SKOR toffee bar, chopped into bits

1 Preheat the oven to 350 degrees. Grease an 8-inch square pan and line it with two criss-crossed sheets of parchment leaving a 2-inch overhang on each side. Set aside.

2 Toast the walnuts on a sheet tray for 6 to 7 minutes until fragrant. Set aside to cool.

3 Brown the butter: In a small saucepan over medium heat, boil the butter, stirring constantly until browned, about 2 minutes. Pour into the bowl of an electric mixer fitted with the paddle attachment. Cream the browned butter and sugars on medium speed for 2 minutes. Add the egg and vanilla extract. Mix on medium speed until combined. Add the flour, salt, walnuts, chocolate chunks, and toffee bits. Mix on low speed until all ingredients are incorporated.

4 Spread the batter into the prepared pan and smooth out the top. Bake for 20 to 25 minutes until a toothpick comes out relatively clean. Do not overbake. Let cool completely at room temperature before cutting.

For a delicious alternative, try substituting chopped smokehouse almonds for the walnuts.

sunbursts ★

Makes about 8 sandwich cookies

I am extremely fortunate to live in an area where the sun typically shines at least 70 percent of the year. Like a shot of the sun's rays, this tender cookie and bright orange filling will awaken you with just one bite. At Sugar Blossom, a customer recently came in and bought one of these Sunburst cookies. She walked out the door while taking a bite of the cookie. I watched her stop in her tracks, turn around, and head right back into the shop. I was worried for a minute until I saw the smile on her face. She exclaimed, "That's the most amazing cookie I've ever tasted," and then bought every Sunburst we had left.

1 cup (2 sticks) unsalted butter, at room temperature

¼ cup sugar

¼ cup powdered sugar, sifted

1 large egg

1 teaspoon pure vanilla extract

1½ cups all-purpose flour

¾ teaspoon baking powder

¼ teaspoon salt

Powdered sugar for sprinkling

1 cup orange marmalade

1 Preheat the oven to 375 degrees. Line a cookie tray with parchment paper or aluminum foil.

2 In a mixer fitted with the paddle attachment, cream the butter and sugars on medium speed until light and fluffy, about 1 minute. Add egg and vanilla, and beat for another minute until combined. On low speed, beat in the flour, baking powder, and salt. Wrap the dough in plastic and chill in refrigerator for at least 30 minutes.

3 On a floured surface, roll out the dough to ¼ inch thick. Using a 3-inch fluted cutter, cut out cookies and place an inch apart on prepared tray. Using a smaller 1-inch fluted cutter, cut out centers in half of the cookies. Re-roll any scraps and repeat steps. (Note: If the cookies get soft, place the tray with the unbaked cookies in the refrigerator for about 10 minutes to chill the dough. This will prevent the cookies from losing their shape when baked.)

4 Bake the cookies for 6 to 7 minutes, or until bottoms are lightly browned. Remove tray from oven and let cool completely at room temperature.

5 To assemble the cookie sandwiches, place the top cookies (the ones with the center hole) on a tray and dust with powdered sugar. Flip the remaining whole cookies over and spread marmalade on them. Place the sugared cookies on top of the marmalade and gently sandwich the cookies together. Fill the open centers with an additional dab of marmalade.

hand-crafted ice cream sandwiches

Ice cream is America's most popular summertime treat, especially by the beach. The simplest, no-waste way to enjoy ice cream is with an edible sweet such as a wafer, macaron, or cone among other things. My favorite way is as an ice cream sandwich. You get the perfect ratio of cookie to ice cream in every bite and you can create countless flavor combinations. These days, there are so many different ice cream flavors available at the grocery store that you can customize your ice cream sandwich any way you choose.

For my ice cream sandwiches, I like to bake cake-like sheet cookies. They stay soft even when frozen, making them most similar to the ice cream sandwiches from when I grew up. Also, as you'll see, they are easy to make. They bake and cool quickly and one recipe yields eight ice cream sandwiches, leaving you with extras that can be stored in the freezer for your weekend beach gatherings. Last but not least, thanks to time in the freezer, the ice cream firms up nicely so you can enjoy the sandwich without making a mess.

classic

Makes 8 sandwiches

½ cup (1 stick) unsalted butter, at room temperature

½ cup sugar

1 large egg

½ cup all-purpose flour

¼ cup unsweetened cocoa powder

½ teaspoon baking powder

1½ to 2 quarts store-bought vanilla ice cream

This is the flavor pairing that started it all and sometimes simple is better. Chocolate and vanilla combine to make one of the all-time best ice cream treats.

1 Preheat the oven to 350 degrees. Grease a 13x18-inch rimmed baking sheet and line the bottom with parchment paper or aluminum foil, leaving a 2-inch overhang on the two shorter sides.

2 In a mixer fitted with the paddle attachment, mix the butter and sugar on medium speed until light and fluffy, about 1 minute. Beat in the egg. Add the flour, cocoa powder, and baking powder. Mix until incorporated, about 1 minute more. Make sure to scrape the bowl to ensure ingredients are fully combined.

3 Using a mini offset spatula, spread the batter evenly in the prepared pan. Make sure to smooth the top. Bake for 8 minutes. Remove from oven and let cool completely in the refrigerator.

4 After the cake has completely cooled, gently remove it from the pan and invert it onto a cutting board. Remove the parchment, cut the cake in half, and place one of the halves on a large piece of foil.

5 Remove the ice cream from the freezer and transfer to a mixer fitted with the paddle attachment. Start at low speed and continue mixing until it reaches the consistency of soft-serve ice cream. Using a mini offset spatula, spread the ice cream over the cake half that is on the foil. Slide the other cake half off the cutting board and onto the ice cream. Press down gently. Wrap the foil up and around the assembled dessert. Place in the freezer at least 3 hours or overnight.

6 When ice cream is fully set, remove the dessert from the freezer and trim the edges if necessary. Cut the rectangle into 8 equal pieces. Individually wrap each ice cream sandwich with parchment paper, wax paper, or aluminum foil and tape to seal. Store the sandwiches in an airtight container in the freezer for up to a week.

waimea bay ★

Makes 8 sandwiches

On the famous North Shore of O'ahu is one of the most well-known surf destinations in the world. Waimea Bay, which means "red water," gets its name from the red soil that washes into the bay from the valleys via Waimea River. Every winter some of the largest waves are recorded here and surfers flock to take on these mighty red swells. These giant waves of red water inspired me to create this red velvet ice cream sandwich.

1 Preheat the oven to 350 degrees. Grease a 13x18-inch rimmed baking sheet and line the bottom with parchment paper or aluminum foil, leaving a 2-inch overhang on the two shorter sides.

2 In a mixer fitted with the paddle attachment, mix the butter and sugar on medium speed until light and fluffy, about 1 minute. Beat in the egg and red food color. Add the flour, cocoa powder, and baking powder. Mix until incorporated, about 1 minute more. Make sure to scrape the bowl to ensure ingredients are fully combined.

3 Using a mini offset spatula, spread the batter evenly in the prepared pan. Make sure to smooth the top. Bake for 8 minutes. Remove from oven and let cool completely in the refrigerator.

4 After the cake has completely cooled, gently remove it from the pan and invert it onto a cutting board. Remove the parchment, cut the cake in half and place one of the halves on a large piece of foil.

5 Remove the ice cream from the freezer and transfer to a mixer fitted with the paddle attachment. Start at low speed and continue mixing until it reaches the consistency of soft-serve ice cream. Using a mini offset spatula, spread the ice cream over the cake half that is on the foil. Slide the other cake half off the cutting board and onto the ice cream. Press down gently. Wrap the foil up and around the assembled dessert. Place in the freezer at least 3 hours or overnight.

6 When ice cream is fully set, remove the dessert from the freezer and trim the edges if necessary. Cut the rectangle into 8 equal pieces. Individually wrap each ice cream sandwich with parchment paper, wax paper, or aluminum foil and tape to seal. Store the sandwiches in an airtight container in the freezer for up to a week.

6 tablespoons (¾ stick) unsalted butter, at room temperature

¾ cup sugar

1 large egg

1 teaspoon red food color

1 cup all-purpose flour

1½ tablespoons unsweetened cocoa powder

1 teaspoon baking powder

1½ to 2 quarts store-bought red velvet ice cream

I love using Blue Bunny Red Carpet Red Velvet ice cream for this sandwich.

st. barths

Makes 8 sandwiches

½ cup (1 stick) unsalted butter, at room temperature

½ cup sugar

1 large egg

1 teaspoon pure vanilla extract

½ cup all-purpose flour

¼ cup unsweetened cocoa powder

½ teaspoon baking powder

¼ teaspoon salt

1½ to 2 quarts store-bought chocolate ice cream

2 cups mini semi-sweet chocolate chips

If you want to get a dark chocolate tan, much like the color of this decadent ice cream sandwich, head to St. Barths. This French island has some of the best sunbathing weather I have ever experienced. Plus, the glistening Caribbean waters provide an amazing backdrop to your sunbathing setup. When you need to cool off from the sun's rays, this island offers exceptional Caribbean cuisine, chic boutiques, and fun beach clubs where you can dance to some of the best DJs in the world.

1 Preheat the oven to 350 degrees. Grease a 13x18-inch rimmed baking sheet and line the bottom with parchment paper or aluminum foil, leaving a 2-inch overhang on the two shorter sides.

2 In a mixer fitted with the paddle attachment, mix the butter and sugar on medium speed until light and fluffy, about 1 minute. Beat in the egg and vanilla. Add the flour, cocoa powder, baking powder, and salt. Mix until incorporated, about 1 minute more. Make sure to scrape the bowl to ensure ingredients are fully combined.

3 Using a mini offset spatula, spread the batter evenly in the prepared pan. Make sure to smooth the top. Bake for 8 minutes. Remove from oven and let cool completely in the refrigerator.

4 After the cake has completely cooled, gently remove it from the pan and invert it onto a cutting board. Remove the parchment, cut the cake in half, and place one of the halves on a large piece of foil.

5 Remove the ice cream from the freezer and transfer to a mixer fitted with the paddle attachment. Start at low speed and continue mixing until it reaches the consistency of soft-serve ice cream. Using a mini offset spatula, spread the ice cream over the cake half that is on the foil. Slide the other cake half off the cutting board and onto the ice cream. Wrap the foil up and around the assembled dessert. Place in the freezer at least 3 hours or overnight.

6 When ice cream is fully set, remove the dessert from the freezer, and trim the edges if necessary. Cut the rectangle into 8 equal pieces. Pile the chocolate chips on a plate. Coat the edges of the ice cream sandwiches with the chocolate chips by gently pressing each side into the pile of chips. Individually wrap each ice cream sandwich with parchment paper, wax paper, or aluminum foil and tape to seal. Store the sandwiches in an airtight container in the freezer for up to a week.

malibu

Makes 8 sandwiches

After seeing the final design of this delicious ice cream sandwich, I could think of no better moniker for it than Malibu. This affluent beach community of Los Angeles County is home to many celebrities and bigwigs in the entertainment industry. Like the sugar-coated sides of this cinnamon ice cream sandwich, everything just seems to sparkle a little brighter in Malibu.

½ cup (1 stick) unsalted butter, at room temperature

½ cup sugar

1 large egg

¾ cup all-purpose flour

1 teaspoon baking powder

½ teaspoon ground cinnamon

1½ to 2 quarts store-bought vanilla ice cream

1½ teaspoons ground cinnamon

2 cups white sparkling sugar

1 Preheat the oven to 350 degrees. Grease a 13x18-inch rimmed baking sheet and line the bottom with parchment paper or aluminum foil, leaving a 2-inch overhang on the two shorter sides.

2 In a mixer fitted with the paddle attachment, mix the butter and sugar on medium speed until light and fluffy, about 1 minute. Beat in the egg. Add the flour, baking powder, and cinnamon. Mix until incorporated, about 1 minute more. Make sure to scrape the bowl to ensure ingredients are fully combined.

3 Using a mini offset spatula, spread the batter evenly in the prepared pan. Make sure to smooth the top. Bake for 8 minutes. Remove from oven and let cool completely in the refrigerator.

4 After the cake has completely cooled, gently remove it from the pan and invert it onto a cutting board. Remove the parchment, cut the cake in half, and place one of the halves on a large piece of foil.

5 Remove the ice cream from the freezer and transfer to a mixer fitted with the paddle attachment. Add the cinnamon. Start at low speed and continue mixing until it reaches the consistency of soft-serve ice cream. Using a mini offset spatula, spread the ice cream over the cake half that is on the foil. Slide the other cake half off the cutting board and onto the ice cream. Wrap the foil up and around the assembled dessert. Place in the freezer at least 3 hours or overnight.

6 When ice cream is fully set, remove the dessert from the freezer and trim the edges if necessary. Cut the rectangle into 8 equal pieces. Pile the sparkling sugar on a plate. Coat the edges of the ice cream sandwiches with the sugar by gently pressing each side into the pile of sugar. Individually wrap each ice cream sandwich with parchment paper, wax paper, or aluminum foil and tape to seal. Store the sandwiches in an airtight container in the freezer for up to a week.

La Jolla

Makes 8 sandwiches

6 tablespoons (¾ stick) unsalted butter, at room temperature

¼ cup smooth peanut butter

½ cup sugar

1 large egg

½ teaspoon pure vanilla extract

½ cup all-purpose flour

¼ cup unsweetened cocoa powder

½ teaspoon baking powder

½ teaspoon salt

1½ to 2 quarts store-bought vanilla ice cream

½ cup smooth peanut butter

1 Butterfinger candy bar, finely chopped

Just north of San Diego, California, is a short stretch of land that curves along the coast of the Pacific Ocean. This "jewel" of San Diego is the beach town of La Jolla and has often been described as having a European resort atmosphere with California fun. One of my favorite things to do here is spend the early morning kayaking the famous and beautiful La Jolla cove. I like to spend the remainder of the day exploring the many peaceful trails of Torrey Pines State Reserve. Many of the trails lead to gorgeous, unspoiled beaches. After a full day outdoors, I am more than ready to devour this decadent chocolate peanut butter ice cream sandwich.

1 Preheat the oven to 350 degrees. Grease a 13x18-inch rimmed baking sheet and line the bottom with parchment paper or aluminum foil, leaving a 2-inch overhang on the two shorter sides.

2 In a mixer fitted with the paddle attachment, mix the butter, peanut butter, and sugar on medium speed until light and fluffy, about 1 minute. Beat in the egg and vanilla. Add the flour, cocoa powder, baking powder, and salt. Mix until incorporated, about 1 minute more. Make sure to scrape the bowl to ensure ingredients are fully combined.

3 Using a mini offset spatula, spread the batter evenly in the prepared pan. Make sure to smooth the top. Bake for 10 minutes. Remove from oven and let cool completely in the refrigerator.

4 After the cake has completely cooled, gently remove it from the pan and invert it onto a cutting board. Remove the parchment, cut the cake in half, and place one of the halves on a large piece of foil.

5 Remove the ice cream from the freezer and transfer to a mixer fitted with the paddle attachment. Add the peanut butter. Start at low speed and continue mixing until it reaches the consistency of soft-serve ice cream. Using a mini offset spatula, spread the ice cream over the cake half that is on the foil. Slide the other cake half off the cutting board and onto the ice cream. Wrap the foil up and around the assembled dessert. Place in the freezer at least 3 hours or overnight.

6 When ice cream is fully set, remove the dessert from the freezer and trim the edges if necessary. Cut the rectangle into 8 equal pieces. Pile the chopped Butterfinger pieces on a dinner plate. Coat the edges of the ice cream sandwiches by gently pressing each side into the pile of candy. Individually wrap each ice cream sandwich with parchment paper, wax paper, or aluminum foil and tape to seal. Store the sandwiches in an airtight container in the freezer for up to a week.

nantucket

Makes 8 sandwiches

When thinking of a name for this delicious espresso banana sandwich, I immediately thought of Nantucket. This banana-shaped island off the coast of Massachusetts is a summer retreat for many beach lovers like me. Choose to ride your bike along the many winding paths on the island and stop at different beaches along the way. With historic sites, quaint inns, and unique dining options such as chowder shacks and sunset clam bakes, Nantucket has something for everyone.

½ cup (1 stick) unsalted butter, at room temperature

½ cup sugar

1 large egg

1 teaspoon pure vanilla extract

¾ cup all-purpose flour

1 tablespoon Medaglia D'oro instant espresso

1 teaspoon baking powder

¼ teaspoon salt

1½ to 2 quarts store-bought vanilla ice cream

2 large bananas, very ripe and mashed

1 Preheat the oven to 350 degrees. Grease a 13x18-inch rimmed baking sheet and line the bottom with parchment paper or aluminum foil, leaving a 2-inch overhang on the two shorter sides.

2 In a mixer fitted with the paddle attachment, mix the butter and sugar on medium speed until light and fluffy, about 1 minute. Beat in the egg and vanilla. Add the flour, espresso, baking powder, and salt. Mix until incorporated, about 1 minute more. Make sure to scrape the bowl to ensure ingredients are fully combined.

3 Using a mini offset spatula, spread the batter evenly in the prepared pan. Make sure to smooth the top. Bake for 10 minutes. Remove from oven and let cool completely in the refrigerator.

4 After the cake has completely cooled, gently remove it from the pan and invert it onto a cutting board. Remove the parchment, cut the cake in half and place one of the halves on a large piece of foil.

5 Remove the ice cream from the freezer and transfer to a mixer fitted with the paddle attachment. Add the mashed bananas. Start at low speed and continue mixing until it reaches the consistency of soft-serve ice cream. Using a mini offset spatula, spread the ice cream over the cake half that is on the foil. Slide the other cake half off the cutting board and onto the ice cream. Wrap the foil up and around the assembled dessert. Place in the freezer at least 3 hours or overnight.

6 When ice cream is fully set, remove the dessert from the freezer and trim the edges if necessary. Cut the rectangle into 8 equal pieces. Individually wrap each ice cream sandwich with parchment paper, wax paper, or aluminum foil and tape to seal. Store the sandwiches in an airtight container in the freezer for up to a week.

dulce del mar ★

Makes 8 sandwiches

½ cup (1 stick) unsalted butter, at room temperature

½ cup sugar

¼ cup light brown sugar

1 large egg

½ teaspoon pure vanilla extract

1 cup all-purpose flour

1 teaspoon baking powder

1 teaspoon salt

¼ cup walnuts, finely chopped

1 (13.4-ounce) can Nestle La Lechera Dulce de Leche

1½ to 2 quarts store-bought vanilla ice cream

In my attempts to use homemade dulce de leche, the product was a bit too runny for my liking. I had the best results with the Nestle brand.

This may be my favorite ice cream sandwich. I love the sweet salty combination of the dulce de leche and walnut cookie. Del Mar, a beautiful beachside community in San Diego County, California, boasts another combination that I love. It is home to the famous Del Mar racetrack, founded in 1937 by a group of Hollywood royalty including Bing Crosby and Gary Cooper, as a home for top level thoroughbred racing. It's a small community less than two square miles with a beautiful stretch of beach and spectacular homes overlooking the racetrack and its fairgrounds. Del Mar's combination of beach and racetrack makes this a destination worth seeking out when visiting Southern California.

1 Preheat the oven to 350 degrees. Grease a 13×18-inch rimmed baking sheet and line the bottom with parchment paper or aluminum foil, leaving a 2-inch overhang on the two shorter sides.

2 In a mixer fitted with the paddle attachment, mix the butter and sugars on medium speed until light and fluffy, about 1 minute. Beat in the egg and vanilla. Add the flour, baking powder, and salt. Mix until incorporated, about 1 minute more. Make sure to scrape the bowl to ensure ingredients are fully combined.

3 Using a mini offset spatula, spread the batter evenly in the prepared pan. Make sure to smooth the top. Sprinkle the chopped walnuts over the batter, pressing them down into the batter. Bake for 10 minutes. Remove from oven and let cool completely in the refrigerator.

4 After the cake has completely cooled, gently remove it from the pan and invert it onto a cutting board. Remove the parchment, cut the cake in half, and place one of the halves on a large piece of foil, walnut-side down. Using a mini offset spatula, spread the dulce de leche evenly on each half.

5 Remove the ice cream from the freezer and transfer to a mixer fitted with the paddle attachment. Start at low speed and continue mixing until it reaches the consistency of soft-serve ice cream. Using a mini offset spatula, spread the ice cream over the cake half that is on the foil. Flip the other cake half off the cutting board and onto the ice cream. Wrap the foil up and around the assembled dessert. Place in the freezer at least 3 hours or overnight.

6 When ice cream is fully set, remove the dessert from the freezer and trim the edges if necessary. Cut the rectangle into 8 equal pieces. Individually wrap each ice cream sandwich with parchment paper, wax paper, or aluminum foil and tape to seal. Store the sandwiches in an airtight container in the freezer for up to a week.

frozen pops

I really enjoyed working on this chapter. Probably because by the time I started developing these recipes, it was the heart of summer and turning on my oven at the beach house was the last thing I wanted to do. Let's just say I was happy to give my oven a break.

In this chapter, I share recipes for all sorts of frozen pops including fruit pops, chocolate pops, and creamy pops made with dairy. Frozen pops are a great summertime treat to make when you're at a beach house and expecting a wave of beachgoers to need a refreshing treat in the middle of the day. They are easy to make and don't require many tools. Aside from the ingredients, the main tools you will need are a blender, saucepan, strainer, stirring and cutting utensils, some molds, and popsicle sticks.

I developed these recipes using fresh fruit rather than frozen. I also used fresh fruit juices in the recipes that called for it. While frozen fruit may be the only option for some of you, I highly recommend that you use fresh whenever possible.

There are many types of containers that can be used as frozen pop molds. While at the beach, an easy and cheap option is the Dixie cup. It is the perfect portion size for such a sweet treat and, after a quick rinse under warm water, the Dixie cup easily releases the frozen pop. I also like using party cups—you know, those small paper cups used for serving snacks such as nuts. For sticks, I use old-fashioned wooden sticks, which can be found at craft stores. I've also found that lollipop sticks work well.

To unmold your frozen pops, simply let them sit on the counter for a few minutes before releasing, or if you're in a hurry, run the mold under warm tap water to slightly melt the pop and loosen it from the mold.

I've done my best to create delicious pops that not only taste good, but also are attractive. I hope they provide you with a sweet way to cool off during your day at the beach. Enjoy!

watermelon gv

Makes about 4 cups

2 pounds seedless watermelon flesh, about ½ a small melon

3 tablespoons agave nectar

Pinch of salt

I'm not sure if there's a more iconic sign of summer at the beach than cold slices of watermelon, especially frozen watermelon. A watermelon is more than 90 percent water by weight, which makes it the perfect fruit to hydrate you on a hot day at the beach. It is also the perfect fruit to use in making a frozen pop. It doesn't take much sugar to sweeten these pops and, in fact, I like to use agave nectar in place of sugar to sweeten them.

1 Chop the watermelon flesh into medium cubes and add about a third to the blender. Pulse until puréed. Add the remaining watermelon in thirds, blending after each addition. Add the agave and salt. Process until the mixture is completely smooth.

2 Divide the mixture among your pop molds. Freeze until partially frozen and then insert sticks. Freeze until solid, at least 4 hours or overnight.

peach green tea ᵍᵛ

Makes about 2 cups

Sweet peach and mild earthy green tea combine to make this delicious frozen treat. Even better, you can enjoy the health benefits of green tea while savoring this frozen pop. We can all thank China for introducing us to the wonders of green tea. In southern China, close to the Vietnam border, lies Beihai City, home to Silver Beach. It is named for its soft, glittery quartz sand that shines like silver under the sun. Imagine yourself on Silver Beach for a hot day of diving, boating, or just laying out. Right on time, someone from up the beach brings a cooler filled with freezing cold Peach Green Tea pops and you smile at what is now a perfect day.

2 ripe yellow peaches
One medium ice bath
1 cup water
2 tablespoons sugar
2 bags green tea

1 *Peel and pit the peaches:* Score the pointed tip of the peaches with an X using a sharp paring knife. Bring a pot of water to a low boil over medium heat. Submerge the peaches in the water for about 1 minute (the less ripe, the more time you will need to boil them). Remove the peaches and dunk them in an ice bath until completely cool. Gently peel the peaches by pulling at the skin by the scored X or rubbing it off gently with your thumb. If the skin does not come off easily, repeat the boiling and cooling steps again. Using a sharp knife, slice the peaches in half and gently remove the pits. Add the peaches to the blender.

2 Bring 1 cup water to a boil in a small saucepan. Remove from the heat and stir in the sugar. Add the tea bags and let steep for 3 minutes. Remove and discard the tea bags and pour the tea over the peaches in the blender. Process the mixture until completely smooth.

3 Divide the mixture among your pop molds. Freeze until partially frozen and then insert sticks. Freeze until solid, at least 4 hours or overnight.

pineapple strawberry tarragon [gv]

Makes about 2½ cups

1 pineapple, about 3 pounds

2 cups water

3 grams tarragon leaves

One small ice bath

2 tablespoons clover honey

⅓ cup orange juice (about 1 large orange)

1 tablespoon lime juice (about ½ a lime)

1 tablespoon sugar

4 ounces strawberries, hulled and halved (about 10 small strawberries)

While tarragon is mostly seen in savory recipes, I love to use it (along with other herbs) in my desserts. Herbs add a unique twist on sweets that surprise the palate. Here the tarragon lends a faint hint of licorice that blends well with the acidic pineapple and is rounded out with the sweetness of strawberries.

1 Peel the pineapple with a sharp knife and cut off the flesh around the core. Chop the flesh into medium cubes and place in the blender.

2 Bring the water to a rolling boil in a medium saucepan. Add the tarragon leaves and boil for 30 seconds. Remove the leaves with a strainer and quickly blanch them in the ice bath for 10 seconds. Remove the leaves and squeeze any excess water from them. Add them to the blender along with the honey. Process until smooth. Pulse in the orange juice, lime juice, and sugar. Add the strawberries and process the mixture until completely smooth.

3 Divide the mixture among your pop molds. Freeze until partially frozen and then insert sticks. Freeze until solid, at least 4 hours or overnight.

champagne raspberry gv ⏰ ★

Makes about 3 cups

This may be my favorite of the frozen pops in this book. I love champagne on its own, but the addition of raspberry and sugar turns it into a delicious frozen treat that goes down a little too easily!

1 Combine the sugar and water in a small saucepan over high heat. Bring to a boil for 1 minute. Stir in the honey and remove from the heat.

2 Add the raspberries to the blender. Pour the simple syrup over the berries and turn the blender on high speed for 30 seconds to purée the mixture. Pour the raspberry mixture through a strainer fitted over a clean bowl to remove the seeds. Discard the seeds. Stir in the lime juice and the champagne.

3 Divide the mixture among your pop molds. Freeze until partially frozen and then insert sticks. Freeze until solid, at least 4 hours or overnight.

½ cup sugar

½ cup water

1 teaspoon clover honey

2 (6-ounce) packages raspberries

2 tablespoons lime juice (1 lime)

1 cup champagne, opened about 30 minutes prior to using

citrus lemongrass *gv*

Makes about 1 cup

2 lemongrass stalks

1⅓ cups tangerine juice
(10 to 11 tangerines)

⅓ cup lemon juice
(2 to 3 lemons)

¼ cup lime juice (2 to 3 limes)

2 tablespoons + 2 teaspoons
sugar

Pinch of salt

Combining lemongrass with citrus fruits such as tangerines, lemons, and limes produces a refreshing frozen pop that makes a perfect palate cleanser after a delicious beach meal. To those who are not familiar with lemongrass, it is a tropical lemon-scented grass used frequently in Thai cuisine. On your voyage to Thailand, get ready to see scores of beautiful beaches all along its coast. It would be hard to name the most beautiful beach in this country, but one of my favorites is Railay Beach in southern Thailand. Take a water taxi to this gorgeous beach surrounded by lush jungle and the warm Andaman Sea. I suggest staying late and watching the sun set between the huge limestone formations that rise out of the sea.

1 Rinse the lemongrass stalks well. Cut off the lower bulb and remove the tough outer leaves. Cut the stalks in half. Using a meat pounder, "bruise" the lemongrass to break up the stalks and release their oils. Place into a medium saucepan. Add the tangerine, lemon, and lime juices along with the sugar and salt.

Bring to a boil and then remove from heat. Let steep for 5 minutes. Strain the juice.

2 Divide the mixture among your pop molds. Freeze until partially frozen and then insert sticks. Freeze until solid, at least 4 hours or overnight.

strawberry gv

This frozen pop is simple to make and its bright red color makes it impossible to ignore. Using in-season, farmers' market strawberries is the way to go with this frozen pop. The lime and orange juices add vibrancy while the salt enhances all the flavors.

1 pound fresh strawberries

½ teaspoon lime juice (1 lime wedge)

Pinch of salt

⅓ cup sugar

¼ cup orange juice (1 large orange)

1 Clean, hull, and halve the strawberries. Place in the blender along with the lime juice and pinch of salt.

2 In a small saucepan, bring the sugar and orange juice to a simmer over medium heat and stir until sugar is dissolved. Remove from heat and pour over the strawberries in the blender. Process until the mixture is completely smooth.

3 Divide the mixture among your pop molds. Freeze until partially frozen and then insert sticks. Freeze until solid, at least 4 hours or overnight.

caramelized banana fudgsicles

Makes about 2 cups

½ cup sugar

½ cup water

1 cup half–and–half

1 ripe medium banana, mashed (about ½ cup)

⅓ cup milk chocolate chips

This smooth milk chocolate frozen pop is heavenly. The caramelized banana gives this pop depth and sweetness. It's gourmet pudding on a stick!

1 Combine the sugar and water in a small, clean saucepan over medium-high heat. Bring to a boil and cook until the sugar turns a dark amber. Remove from the heat and slowly whisk in the half-and-half, followed by the mashed banana. Return the caramel to medium heat and cook until all of the sugar is dissolved. Pour into the blender. Add the milk chocolate chips. Process the mixture until completely smooth.

2 Divide the mixture among your pop molds. Freeze until partially frozen and then insert sticks. Freeze until solid, at least 4 hours or overnight.

mango yogurt swirl

Makes about 3½ cups

Mangoes are native to India, Burma, and the Andaman Islands, a group of archipelagic islands in the Bay of Bengal. Havelock Island, one of the Andamans, is home to Radhanagar Beach, which is often referred to as the most beautiful beach in Asia. Inspired by this gorgeous beach locale, I wanted to make a beautiful frozen pop with a native ingredient that represents the peaceful beauty found on this beach. I created this pop after the mango lassi. What better way to quench your thirst on a hot summer day and relax your mind, body, *and* soul than with a frozen pop version of this favorite Indian beverage.

2 ripe mangos

4 tablespoons + 2 tablespoons sugar

½ cup cold water

1½ cups whole milk yogurt

1 Remove the skin from the mangos and cut the flesh around the seeds. Chop the flesh into small pieces and add to the blender along with 4 tablespoons of the sugar. Pulse until smooth. Add the water and process until completely smooth.

2 Stir the yogurt with the remaining 2 tablespoons of sugar until thoroughly combined. Layer about 3 tablespoons each of the mango purée and yogurt in alternating fashion, beginning and ending with mango, into your pop molds. Freeze until partially frozen and then insert sticks. Freeze until solid, at least 4 hours or overnight.

orange pekoe blackberry gv

Makes about 2 cups

3 ounces ripe blackberries

2 cups water

4 teaspoons sugar

½ teaspoon lemon juice

2 orange pekoe tea bags

Orange pekoe is a grade of black tea from southern India and Sri Lanka, an island country in the northern Indian Ocean. Covered with stunning landscapes of tea plantations, botanical gardens, pristine beaches, and waterfalls, Sri Lanka is often referred to as the wonder of Asia. It is a beach lovers' paradise and offers visitors an experience for all the senses. From its unspoiled beaches, captivating cultural heritage, to palate awakening spices in its cuisine, Sri Lanka is a paradise island worth visiting.

1 Rinse and slice the blackberries in half. Set aside.

2 Bring the water to a boil in a small saucepan over high heat. Remove from the heat and stir in the sugar and lemon juice. Add the tea bags and steep for 2 minutes. Remove and discard the tea bags. Do not squeeze the tea bags.

3 Divide the mixture among your pop molds. Drop two blackberry halves into each mold. Freeze until chilled and just beginning to freeze, then drop in the remaining blackberries. Continue freezing the pops until partially frozen and insert sticks. Freeze until solid, at least 4 hours or overnight.

pies, crisps, a cobbler, and a cheesecake

While contemplating which recipes to create for this book, it was clear to me that pies had to play a central role. Everyone has their favorite, probably from when they were little. My goal was to create delicious and unique recipes that would reinvigorate your desire to roll out some pie dough, pick up some fresh seasonal fruit, and create something delicious and wonderful.

So what makes a good pie? The simple straightforward answer is a great crust and great filling. The crust should be distinct from the filling, have a golden color, and buttery flavor. Fruit fillings should be mostly fruit with just a small amount of liquid that after baking isn't runny or too gelatinous. Custards should be firm enough to keep their shape when sliced, yet not too firm that they jiggle.

In this section, I've included recipes for fruit and custard pies. My all-time favorite is the apple pie . . . as traditional as it gets. I've included my unique twist on this classic pie. By combining apples with ginger and pears in my **Apple and Ginger and Pear, Oh My!** pie (page 168) and topping it with a butter crumble, I created a delicious beach house take on the classic.

All of the recipes in this section were tested with fresh, in-season fruit. Some of you may not have access to fresh fruit year round. If you use frozen fruit in the recipes, please be aware that the recipes may need to be modified by lengthening the baking time or increasing the thickener (e.g. corn starch or flour).

sweet butter crust

Makes one 9-inch crust

1½ cups all-purpose flour

1½ teaspoons sugar

⅛ teaspoon salt

¾ cup (1½ sticks) unsalted butter, very cold and cut into ½-inch cubes

4½ tablespoons ice cold water

This is my go-to crust recipe for most of the pies that I make. It browns nicely in the oven and I love seeing the layers of flaky pastry along the edges when I pull a pie out of the oven. This dough can be made ahead of time and kept in the refrigerator or placed in the freezer for longer storage. I like to add a little bit of sugar to my pie crust to not only add flavor, but also assist in the browning. If you are making a double crust pie, make sure to double this recipe.

1 In a mixer fitted with the paddle attachment, mix the flour, sugar, and salt. Add the cold cubed butter. Mix on low to medium speed until butter is broken down to pea size, about 1 minute. Add the cold water all at once and mix until the dough comes together, about 15 seconds. Remove dough from the mixer and gently shape it into a disc with your hands. You should be able to see little bits of butter in the dough. Wrap the disc in plastic wrap and refrigerate at least 1 hour and up to 2 days. Freeze for longer storage.

2 Remove dough from the refrigerator. Roll out on a lightly floured surface to a 12-inch circle, about ⅛-inch thick. Place crust into a 9-inch pie plate. Press the dough evenly into the bottom and sides of the pie plate. For a *single* pie crust, use kitchen scissors to trim the dough leaving a ½-inch overhang. Fold overhang under to be flush with edge of pie plate. Flute as desired. For a *double* pie crust, use kitchen scissors to trim the dough flush with the edge of the pie plate. Roll out the second disc on a lightly floured surface to a 12-inch circle, about ⅛-inch thick. Place over the filled pie. Trim edges of dough leaving a ½-inch overhang. Fold top edge under the bottom crust. Press edges together to seal and flute as desired.

chocolate teddy graham crust

Makes one 9-inch crust

On a trip down the cookie aisle at my local market, I had an epiphany. The thought of surgically removing the vanilla cream from the middle of thirty or so Oreos led me to a simpler solution. How could I have forgotten my cherished Teddy Grahams? When pulverized in a food processor and combined with a little sugar and melted butter, these little crunchy guys create a delicious and crunchy chocolate crust that rivals any chocolate cookie crust out there.

2 cups Chocolate Teddy Grahams

1 tablespoon sugar

¼ cup (½ stick) unsalted butter, melted

1 Preheat the oven to 350 degrees.

2 Pulverize the Teddy Grahams in a food processor or coffee grinder. Make sure they are finely crushed. Place them in a large bowl along with the sugar and melted butter. Mix with your hands until incorporated.

3 Transfer mixture to a 9-inch pie pan and press evenly against the bottom and sides of the pan.

4 Bake for 10 minutes. Let the crust cool completely before filling.

graham crust

Makes one 9-inch crust

1½ cups graham crumbs
⅓ cup sugar
¼ cup (½ stick) unsalted butter, melted

This recipe makes a tender graham cracker crust. It is the perfect shell for my custard pies such as the **Chocolate Peanut Butter** (page 188) and **Banana Cream Pies** (page 172).

1 Preheat oven to 350 degrees.

2 Combine the graham crumbs and sugar in a medium bowl. Mix in the melted butter with your hands.

3 Place mixture in a 9-inch pie pan and press crumbs evenly against the bottom and sides of the pan.

4 Bake for 8 to 10 minutes or until the edges begin to brown. Let the crust cool completely before filling.

how to make a lattice pie crust

Step 1. Roll out dough on a lightly floured surface to a 12-inch circle, about ⅛-inch thick. Using a sharp knife or pizza wheel, cut the dough into 9 even strips, about ¾-inch wide.

Step 2. Lay out 5 parallel strips of the pie dough on top of the filling, spacing them equally apart.

Step 3. Fold back the first, third, and fifth strips.

Step 4. Place one long strip of dough perpendicular to the parallel strips. Place it just off center of the pie. Unfold the folded strips over the perpendicular strip.

Step 5. Fold back the second and fourth strips. Lay down a second perpendicular strip of dough about 1 inch apart from the first strip.

Step 6. Unfold the folded strips over the perpendicular strip.

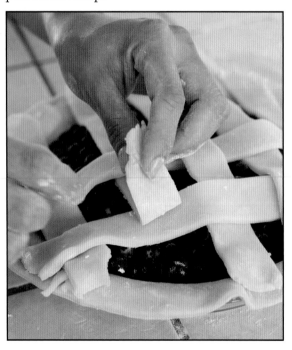

Step 7. On the other half of the pie, fold back the second and fourth strips. Lay down a perpendicular strip of dough about 1 inch apart from the first strip.

Step 8. Unfold the folded strips over the perpendicular strip.

Step 9. Fold back the first, third, and fifth strips. Lay down a perpendicular strip of dough about 1 inch apart from the last one.

Step 10. Unfold the folded strips over the perpendicular strip.

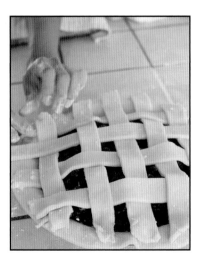

Step 11. Trim the edges of the strips flush with the underlying dough.

Step 12. Fold edges and crimp to secure.

apple jack crisp

Makes one 9x13-inch crisp

Sometimes two great things are even better together. Take one of the most popular fruits, a crispy and juicy apple, and combine it with one of the most popular adult beverages on the planet, Jack Daniel's. The sweetness of the apple blends perfectly with the mellow butterscotch and honey caramel notes of whiskey to create a sublime dessert.

9 large Fuji apples

¼ cup water

3 tablespoons Jack Daniel's Old No. 7

1 teaspoon ground cinnamon

1½ cups rolled oats

1½ cups all-purpose flour

1½ cups light brown sugar

¼ teaspoon baking powder

¼ teaspoon baking soda

1 cup (2 sticks) unsalted butter, melted

1 Preheat the oven to 350 degrees.

2 Peel, core, and slice the apples into ¼-inch wedges. Place in a large bowl and toss with the water, whiskey, and cinnamon. Set aside.

3 In another large bowl, combine the oats, flour, sugar, baking powder, and baking soda and mix until combined. Drizzle the melted butter over the oat mixture and use your hands to mix all the ingredients well. Measure out 1 cup of the mixture and add it to the apple slices. Toss well and transfer apple mixture to a 9x13-inch baking pan. Pack down well. Crumble remaining topping over the apple mixture.

4 Bake for 50 to 55 minutes until juices bubble and topping is lightly browned.

apple and ginger and pear, oh my! ★

Makes one 9-inch pie

1 Sweet Butter Crust
(see page 160)

Crumble

½ cup all-purpose flour

½ cup rolled oats

¼ cup light brown sugar

¼ cup sugar

½ teaspoon ground cinnamon

⅛ teaspoon salt

6 tablespoons (¾ stick)
unsalted butter, cold and cut
into small cubes

Filling

1¼ pounds Fuji apples, peeled
and cut into ¼-inch slices

1¼ pounds Bosc or Anjou
pears, peeled and cut into ¼-
inch slices

¼ cup packed light brown
sugar

¼ cup sugar

1 teaspoon all-purpose flour

1 teaspoon finely grated
peeled fresh ginger

1 tablespoon orange juice

1 teaspoon finely grated
orange zest

⅛ teaspoon salt

3 tablespoons unsalted butter,
at room temperature

My all-time favorite pie has always been apple and this is my beach house version. I added pear to give it depth and extra flavor and added ginger and orange to give it some pop. A delicious butter crumble topping rounds out the pie, giving it great texture.

1 Preheat the oven to 400 degrees. Place a baking sheet in the oven.

2 Prepare 1 Sweet Butter Crust and roll out onto a 9-inch pie pan. Crimp the edges. Place the unbaked pie shell in the refrigerator until needed.

3 *Prepare crumble:* In a mixer fitted with the paddle attachment, combine all the ingredients. Mix on low speed until butter is broken down to pea size. Keep in refrigerator until needed.

4 *Prepare filling:* Cut the apple slices in half. Quarter the pear slices. Place the cut fruit, sugars, flour, ginger, orange juice, zest, and salt in a large bowl and toss to combine. Transfer to a saucepan and cook the fruit over medium heat, stirring frequently, until the fruit is just tender when poked with a fork, but still holds its shape, about 10 to 15 minutes.

5 Transfer to the prepared pie shell, top with butter, and bake on the baking tray for 20 minutes. Remove pie from oven and adjust the oven temperature to 375 degrees. Remove the crumble from the refrigerator and spread over the fruit. Bake for 25 minutes more. Remove from oven and let the pie cool for at least 30 minutes before serving.

ooey gooey pecan tartlets

Makes 4 tartlets (4-inch diameter)

Every year as Thanksgiving would roll around, I would always crave pecan pie, but I hated that most were made with high-fructose corn syrup. I knew that there had to be a way to bake a delicious pecan pie without using a manufactured sweetener. These tartlets are my alternative to the traditional pecan pie. I found that by using maple syrup and honey in place of corn syrup, I was able to create a delicious pecan tart that tasted just as good—if not better—than the kind I had as a kid. My pecan tart has a tender chocolate crust, ooey gooey filling, and crunchy nuts in every bite. Gobble, gobble!

1 Preheat oven to 350 degrees. Grease the bottom and sides of each tartlet shell with pan spray.

2 *Make the filling:* Spread the pecan pieces on an aluminum foil-lined cookie tray. Toast them just until they become aromatic, about 4 to 5 minutes. Remove from oven and set aside to cool.

In a medium saucepan, stir together the butter, sugars, honey, maple syrup, and salt. Place over high heat and boil until the mixture reaches 240 degrees. Remove from heat and pour the mixture into a 2-cup Pyrex measuring cup. Set aside to cool.

3 *Make the crust:* In a mixer fitted with the paddle attachment, cream the butter and sugar until light and fluffy, about 1 minute.

Add the yolk and mix well. Add the flour, cocoa powder, and half–and–half. Beat until incorporated. Transfer the dough to a floured surface and roll it into a small log about 5-inches long. Using a sharp knife, cut the log into 4 equal pieces. Press each piece of dough into the bottom and sides of four tartlet shells. Bake for 8 to 9 minutes, until the surface of the crust is dry. Remove from oven and gently press down the puffed up centers with your fingers.

4 Carefully spread one heaping tablespoon of toasted pecans into each tartlet. Slowly pour the filling into each tartlet as evenly as possible. Let tartlets set up for at least 2 hours before serving.

Filling

4 heaping tablespoons chopped pecans

¼ cup (½ stick) unsalted butter, at room temperature

2 tablespoons sugar

2 tablespoons dark brown sugar

1½ tablespoons clover honey

2 tablespoons Grade A maple syrup

¼ teaspoon salt

Crust

¼ cup (½ stick) unsalted butter, at room temperature

⅓ cup sugar

1 large egg yolk

¾ cup all-purpose flour

2 tablespoons unsweetened cocoa powder

2 tablespoons half-and-half

If you don't have maple syrup, you can substitute with agave nectar.

banana cream pie

Makes one 9-inch pie

1 Graham Crust (see page 162)

Filling

4 tablespoons (2 ounces) dark chocolate, melted

1½ cups whole milk

6 tablespoons sugar

2 tablespoons cornstarch

1 large egg

1 egg yolk

1 teaspoon pure vanilla extract

1 tablespoon unsalted butter, soft

2 medium bananas, ripe

2 cups heavy cream, chilled

1 tablespoon sugar

1 teaspoon pure vanilla extract

Caramel Sauce

¾ cup sugar

¼ cup water

¼ teaspoon lemon juice

½ cup heavy cream

Pinch of salt

Chocolate Curls

¼ cup dark or milk chocolate chips

My take on this classic pie combines all the best components of the many versions of banana cream pie that are out there: chocolate, caramel, graham cracker, vanilla custard, bananas, and whipped cream.

1 Make and bake 1 Graham Crust. Spread melted dark chocolate over the cooled crust. Set aside.

2 *Make the filling:* Combine 1 cup of the milk with 3 tablespoons of the sugar in a medium saucepan over high heat. Bring to a boil and set aside.

In a medium bowl, whisk together the remaining sugar and milk with the cornstarch, egg, and yolk. Whisk in one-third of the hot milk mixture into the egg mixture. Add the egg mixture to the remaining milk in the saucepan. Return the saucepan to medium heat and cook, whisking constantly until pudding boils and thickens, about 2 minutes. Remove from heat and whisk in the vanilla and butter.

3 Pour the hot pudding into the prepared pie shell. Press plastic wrap directly onto the surface of the pudding. Chill until cold, about 4 hours.

4 Thinly slice the bananas and arrange them over the cooled pastry cream. In a mixer fitted with the whip attachment, mix the heavy cream, sugar, and vanilla to stiff peak. Pipe the whipped cream over the banana slices. Garnish with caramel sauce and chocolate curls if desired.

5 *Make the caramel sauce:* Stir together the sugar, water, and lemon juice in a heavy-bottomed small saucepan. Heat the sugar over medium heat until the sugar is dissolved. If necessary, brush the insides of the pan with a wet pastry brush to wash down any crystals sticking to the sides. Increase to high heat and bring to a boil without stirring, until the sugar reaches a deep amber color, about 5 to 7 minutes.

Remove from heat and carefully whisk in the heavy cream. Be careful as the caramel will sputter as the cream is added. If necessary, return to low heat to melt any clumps of caramel. Stir in the salt. Transfer the caramel to a dish, place in the refrigerator, and let cool uncovered.

6 *Make chocolate curls:* Melt the chocolate in the microwave until smooth. Stir occasionally and keep an eye on the chocolate to make sure it doesn't burn. Spread the chocolate onto the back of a clean, flat cookie sheet. The key here is to spread the chocolate as thin as possible. Place the tray in the refrigerator for 5 minutes to set up. Remove the tray from the refrigerator and let stand for 2 to 3 minutes until the chocolate softens slightly and your fingerprint leaves a light imprint.

Using a thin metal spatula (I like to use a fish spatula), scrape the chocolate in a forceful, forward manner and work quickly to make as many curls as you can. If the chocolate gets too soft, simply place tray back into the refrigerator for a minute to harden again. Place the curls on a plate in the refrigerator to harden before using. Store any leftover curls in a Ziploc bag in the freezer.

berry burst pie ★

Makes one 9-inch pie

When I was a kid, my family would often spend Saturdays in the summer picking berries. We'd start early in the morning before it got too hot and humid. At the local farm, they'd give us each a basket, point us to a field, and we'd go out searching for the reddest, plumpest, and juiciest strawberries. Along the sides of the field hanging on fences, blackberries as big as my little hands were waiting to be found. We were only allowed to eat a few, but those warm, ripe berries bursting in my mouth remain one of my favorite memories of summer.

1 *Prepare the pie dough:* Prepare 1 Sweet Butter Crust and roll out onto a 9-inch pie pan. Crimp the edges and poke holes in the bottom of the crust with a fork. Place the unbaked pie shell in the refrigerator until needed.

2 *Prepare the streusel:* Combine all the ingredients in a medium bowl. Vigorously yet gently rub the butter into the dry ingredients with your hands. You want the streusel to resemble loose sand. Store the streusel in the refrigerator until needed.

3 *Prepare the filling:* Preheat the oven to 375 degrees.

Clean, hull, and halve the strawberries. Transfer to a large bowl along with the blackberries, raspberries, and blueberries. In a small bowl, combine the cornstarch, sugar, vanilla, and cinnamon. Sprinkle over the berries and toss to coat.

4 Transfer the berries into the pie shell. Remove the prepared streusel topping from the refrigerator and sprinkle it evenly over the berries.

5 Bake 40 to 45 minutes or until juices bubble through the streusel topping. Let pie set up for at least 3 hours before serving.

1 Sweet Butter Crust
(see page 160)

Streusel
½ cup all-purpose flour

½ cup sugar

½ teaspoon ground cinnamon

¼ cup (½ stick) unsalted butter, at room temperature

Berry filling
10 ounces strawberries

1 (6-ounce) package blackberries

1 (6-ounce) package raspberries

1 (4.4-ounce) package blueberries

4 tablespoons cornstarch

6 tablespoons sugar

½ teaspoon pure vanilla extract

¼ teaspoon ground cinnamon

blueberry lavender pie ★

Makes one 9-inch pie

2 Sweet Butter Crusts (see page 160)

½ cup sugar

3 tablespoons cornstarch

1 teaspoon dried lavender

4 cups fresh blueberries

2 tablespoons unsalted butter, melted

I am a big fan of lavender. In this pie, the floral and citrus notes of lavender blend majestically with the sweet blueberries. As the pie bakes in the oven, the aroma will transport you across the Pacific to the lavender fields on the island of Maui. Created by Agricultural Artist and Horticultural Master Ali'I Chang, Ali'i Kula Lavender Garden is a unique place to visit. Though not native to Hawaii, more than 50,000 lavender plants thrive in this 13.5 acre area of Maui. At an elevation of 4,000 feet, the Lavender Gardens also offer some of the best vistas of the island.

1 Preheat the oven to 400 degrees.

2 Prepare 2 Sweet Butter Crusts. Roll out half of the dough onto a 9-inch pie pan, leaving a ½-inch overhang. Place the unbaked pie shell in the refrigerator until needed. Wrap the remaining dough with plastic wrap and place in refrigerator.

3 Whisk together the sugar, cornstarch, and dried lavender in a large stainless steel bowl. Mix in the blueberries and butter with a rubber spatula. Crush a few berries against the bowl with the back of spatula. Mix until all the berries are coated. Let sit 15 minutes, stirring occasionally.

4 Remove prepared pie shell from refrigerator. Transfer the blueberry mixture into the crust. Form a lattice crust on the pie and crimp the edges decoratively. (See page 163 for step-by-step instructions.) Place pie in freezer for 5 minutes to set up.

5 Bake pie for 40 to 45 minutes or until juices bubble up over the crust.

6 Let pie cool completely at room temperature before serving.

beach house seashore cobbler

Makes one 9-inch sauté or pie pan

3 pounds yellow peaches, ripe

One medium ice bath

½ cup sugar

¼ cup orange juice

1 tablespoon cornstarch

1 large lemon

Biscuit topping

1 cup all-purpose flour

1½ teaspoons baking powder

¼ cup buttermilk

¼ cup vegetable oil

2 tablespoons sugar

2 tablespoons unsalted butter, melted

1 small seashell

I love to serve this cobbler with lemon sorbet or vanilla ice cream.

This may be the most "beachy" recipe in the book. A seashell is pressed into the biscuit topping to remind you of the seashore, it's quick to prepare which will get you out of the kitchen and onto the beach sooner, and its use of fresh juicy peaches is a sure signal that summer is upon us. So get your beach bag out and put your sandals by the door—it's time to go to beach.

1 Preheat the oven to 425 degrees.

2 *Peel and pit the peaches:* Score the pointed tip of the peaches with an X using a sharp paring knife. Bring a pot of water to a low boil over medium heat. Submerge the peaches in the water for about one minute (the less ripe, the more time you will need to boil them). Remove the peaches and dunk them in an ice bath until completely cool. Gently peel the peaches by pulling at the skin by the scored X or rubbing it off gently with your thumb. If the skin does not come off easily, repeat the boiling and cooling steps again. Using a sharp knife, slice the peaches in halves and gently remove the pits. Slice the peaches lengthwise to get 6 to 7 slices per half. Set aside the slices in a large bowl.

3 Whisk together the sugar, orange juice, and cornstarch in a small saucepan. Bring to a boil over medium heat and cook for one minute. Pour the mixture over the peaches and stir to coat the peaches. Transfer peaches to a 9-inch oven-proof sauté pan or 9-inch pie pan. Squeeze the juice of the lemon evenly over the peaches.

4 *Make the topping:* In a mixer fitted with the paddle attachment, mix all the ingredients on medium speed until a smooth dough forms. On a floured surface, pat the dough into an 8-inch circle. Cut into 8 wedges. Press a clean seashell firmly into the dough to transfer the design. Place the wedges over the peaches.

5 Bake for 25 to 28 minutes or until the biscuits feel firm when pressed. Remove from oven and let cool at room temperature.

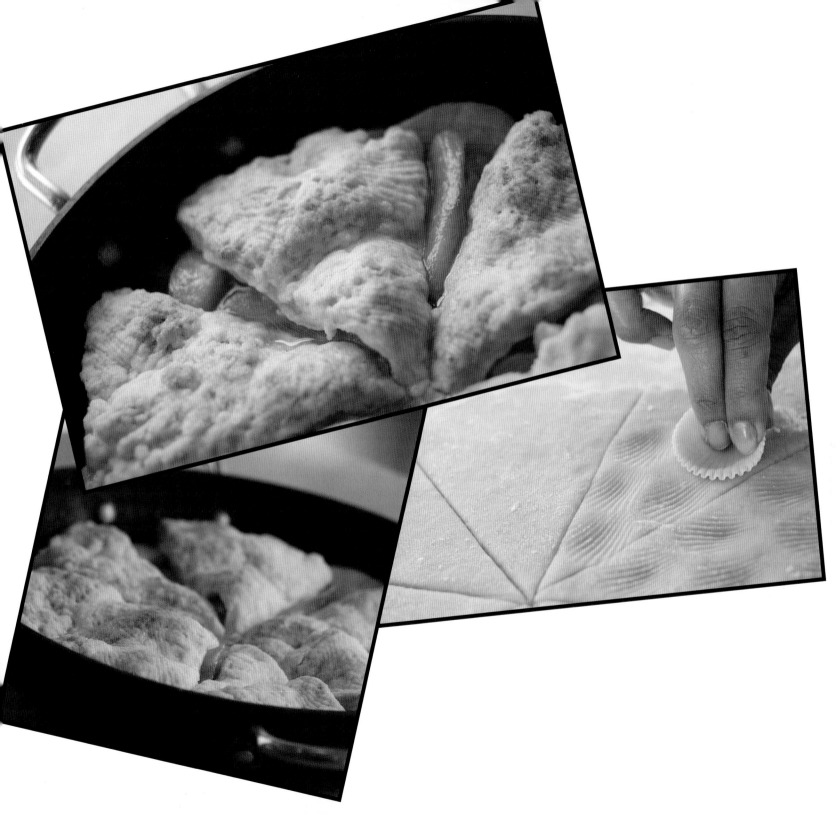

chocolate pillow pie

Makes one 9-inch pie

In the Queensland region of Australia lies Whitehaven Beach, one of the cleanest beaches in the world. At the first glance of its pristine white sand, one can see why it was named by cnn.com as the top Eco Friendly Beach. The bright white sand is due to its high content of pure silica gel. The fact that dogs are not permitted on the beach and smoking is not allowed contributes as well. Much like Whitehaven Beach, the flavor and look of this pie is clean and dazzling. The combination of dark chocolate and sweet vanilla will blow your mind. The billowy whipped cream is the perfect pillow to the luscious and creamy dark chocolate pudding and crunchy crust.

1 Make and bake 1 Chocolate Teddy Graham Crust. Set aside.

2 *Make the filling:* Whisk the egg yolks and cornstarch in a medium bowl and set aside.

Combine the milk, sugar, and salt in a medium saucepan and bring to a simmer over medium heat stirring constantly. Remove from heat.

Whisk in 1 cup of the warm milk mixture into the egg yolks. Pour the yolk mixture back into the saucepan and return to medium heat. Stir constantly until thickened and mixture boils for 30 seconds. Remove from heat, and stir in the chocolate, butter, and vanilla.

Immediately pour pudding into the prepared pie shell, press plastic wrap onto the pudding, and refrigerate at least 4 hours or until pudding is set.

3 *Make the topping:* In a mixer fitted with the whip attachment, whip the heavy cream, sugar, and vanilla extract on high speed until stiff. Pile cream on top of the chocolate pudding, spreading it to the edges of the pie crust while forming

a rounded pillow-like dome. Top with chocolate curl if desired. Refrigerate for at least 1 hour before serving.

4 *Make the chocolate curls:* Melt the chocolate in the microwave until smooth. Stir occasionally and keep an eye on the chocolate to make sure it doesn't burn. Spread the chocolate onto the back of a clean, flat cookie sheet. The key here is to spread the chocolate as thin as possible. Place the tray in the refrigerator for 5 minutes to set up. Remove the tray from the refrigerator and let stand for 2 to 3 minutes until the chocolate softens slightly and your fingerprint leaves a light imprint.

Using a thin metal spatula (I prefer a fish spatula), scrape the chocolate in a forceful, forward manner and work quickly to make as many curls as you can. If the chocolate gets too soft, simply place tray back into the refrigerator for a minute to harden again. Place the curls on a plate in the refrigerator to harden before using. Store any leftover curls in a Ziploc bag in the freezer.

Crust

1 Chocolate Teddy Graham crust (see page 161)

Filling

3 large egg yolks

2 tablespoons cornstarch

1½ cups whole milk

⅓ cup sugar

¼ teaspoon salt

⅔ cup dark chocolate, chopped finely

1 tablespoon unsalted butter, at room temperature

1 teaspoon pure vanilla extract

Topping

2 cups heavy cream, chilled

3 tablespoons sugar

1 teaspoon pure vanilla extract

Chocolate Curls

¼ cup dark or milk chocolate chips

Another delicious garnish for this pie is 1 finely chopped SKOR bar.

windswept cherry pie
Makes one 9-inch pie

1 Sweet Butter Crust
(see page 160)

1 cup cherry cola

2 pounds dark cherries

2 tablespoons cornstarch

6 tablespoons sugar

½ teaspoon lemon juice

¼ teaspoon pure almond
extract

Almond Streusel Topping

¾ cup all-purpose flour

⅓ cup rolled oats

⅓ cup light brown sugar

⅓ cup sliced almonds

¼ cup (½ stick) unsalted
butter, at room temperature

Over the course of 4 to 6 weeks between the months of June and August, Northern Washington State is abuzz. During this time, cherry producers are busy harvesting, packing, and shipping tons of fresh, sweet, and in-season cherries. No doubt that when the season is over, many of them take refuge at Ruby Beach, located in the coastal section of Olympic National Park. The beach gets its name from the ruby-like crystals (a result of past glacier activity) that wash to the beach. As the sun sets, many beachgoers enjoy sitting on the driftwood along the rugged coastline to watch the rays of the setting sun peek through the massive boulders, turning the beach into a sparkling blanket.

1 Preheat oven to 375 degrees.

2 Make 1 Sweet Butter Crust. Roll out the dough over a 9-inch pie dish and crimp the edges. Poke holes in the bottom of the crust with a fork. Place in the refrigerator while you make the filling.

3 *Make the filling:* In a small saucepan over medium heat, bring the cherry cola to a medium bowl. Continue cooking the cola until it is reduced by half. Let the cola cool in the refrigerator while you pit the cherries.

In a medium saucepan, whisk together the reduced cola, cornstarch, sugar, and lemon juice. Bring to a boil over low-medium heat whisking continuously. Add the pitted cherries and continue cooking until mixture is

thickened and shiny, about two minutes. Transfer to a clean bowl and fold in the almond extract. Set aside while you make the oat topping.

4 *Make almond streusel:* Mix together the flour, oats, brown sugar, and almonds in a medium bowl. Add the butter and toss the entire mixture gently with your hands until the butter is incorporated. The mixture will resemble loose cookie dough.

5 Remove the prepared pie crust from the refrigerator. Pour the cherry filling into the shell. Sprinkle the streusel over the filling. Bake for 25 to 35 minutes or until filling bubbles and streusel is golden brown. Let cool completely before serving.

strawberry rhubarb honey crisp ★

Makes one 8-inch square pan

Sometimes delicious desserts are not always about the sweet. A well-orchestrated balance of sweet and tart can take a traditional dessert to the next level. When we take something that is primarily tart in taste such as rhubarb and combine it with perfectly ripe strawberries, a new and remarkable taste emerges. That's what my strawberry rhubarb honey crisp is all about.

12 ounces (about 3 stalks) rhubarb

1 tablespoon orange blossom honey + additional for drizzling

1 tablespoon + ¼ cup sugar

1 pound 6 ounces strawberries, hulled and small-diced

1 tablespoon all-purpose flour

⅛ teaspoon salt

Streusel

¾ cup all-purpose flour

½ cup rolled oats

½ cup sugar

¼ cup light brown sugar

⅛ teaspoon salt

½ cup (1 stick) unsalted butter, very cold

1 Cut the rhubarb stalks in half. Place them in a medium Ziploc freezer bag along with the honey and 1 tablespoon sugar. Seal tightly without air. Fill a medium saucepan with water and bring to a boil over high heat. Once water has boiled for 1 minute, remove from the heat. Drop in the bag of rhubarb and let it "poach" for 25 minutes. Remove bag from water and dry it off well. Lay flat in the refrigerator for at least 4 hours.

2 Preheat the oven to 350 degrees. Lightly butter an 8-inch square baking dish.

3 Remove rhubarb from the bag. Discard the juice. Remove the stringy skin from the stalks and cut the rhubarb into small ½-inch cubes. Transfer the rhubarb to a large bowl and add the diced strawberries, ¼ cup of sugar, flour,

and salt. Mix until incorporated. Set aside the mixture to macerate while you make the streusel.

4 *Make the streusel:* In another large bowl, mix the flour, oats, sugars, and salt until combined. Grate in the cold butter. Mix together with your hands until incorporated. Gently fold in ½ cup of the streusel into the fruit. Transfer the mixture to the prepared baking pan. Top the fruit with the remaining streusel.

5 Bake for 50 minutes in the oven. Turn broiler on and bake for 2 to 3 minutes or until topping is evenly browned. Remove from oven and let cool for at least 5 minutes. Serve with a drizzle of orange blossom honey and vanilla bean ice cream.

candied pumpkin pie

Makes one 9-inch pie

1 Sweet Butter Crust
(see page 160)

Candied pumpkin

1 small (3-pound) pumpkin

4 cups water

2¼ cups light brown sugar

2 teaspoons ground cinnamon

Grated zest of 1 orange

Pie filling

1 (12-ounce) can
evaporated milk

2 large eggs

This is the best version of pumpkin pie I've ever had. The additional step of candying the pumpkin results in a pie that tastes naturally sweet with orange and cinnamon essence. Using fresh pumpkin produces the most wonderfully smooth and creamy custard-like filling you've ever had. I've never gone back to making pumpkin pie any other way.

1 Make 1 Sweet Butter Crust and roll out onto a 9-inch pie pan. Crimp the edges and place the unbaked pie shell in the refrigerator until needed.

2 *Candy the pumpkin:* Cut stem off pumpkin. Cut pumpkin in half. Remove seeds and string. (Optional: Place seeds and string in a bowl of water for later. Use my **Crispy Toasted Pumpkin Seeds** recipe for a nice late-night snack). Cut each half into 4 to 5 wedges. Halve each wedge to get approximately 2-inch long pieces.

3 In a medium saucepan, bring water, brown sugar, cinnamon, and orange zest to a boil over high heat. Reduce the heat to low and add the pumpkin pieces. Simmer for 45 to 60 minutes or until pumpkin is fork tender. Remove from heat and let pumpkin cool in the syrup at room temperature.

4 *Make filling:* Preheat oven to 400 degrees. When pumpkin is cool, remove from syrup and peel off the skin with a sharp knife. Transfer to large bowl. Purée the pumpkin with a blender or food processor. (I use a hand blender.) You can also use the back of a fork if you don't have a blender. Transfer the purée to a sieve. Let sit for 5 minutes to allow excess water to drain.

In a large bowl, whisk the evaporated milk and eggs until combined. Whisk in 2 cups of the pumpkin purée until smooth. (I usually have a couple spoonfuls extra of purée.) Remove pie shell from refrigerator and fill with the pumpkin batter.

5 Bake for 15 minutes. Reduce temperature to 350 degrees. Bake for 50 to 55 minutes or until knife inserted comes out clean. Cool on counter for at least 2 hours before serving.

Just a note about pumpkin varieties. There are many different pumpkin varieties to choose from. Many bakers prefer to use sugar pie pumpkins; however, I use small "jack-o-lantern" pumpkins in this recipe and the results have always been outstanding.

Crispy Toasted Pumpkin Seeds

1 cup raw pumpkin seeds
2 cups water

1 tablespoon + ¼ teaspoon salt
½ teaspoon peanut oil

1 Preheat oven to 375 degrees. Line a baking tray with aluminum foil.

2 Remove string from seeds and discard them. Rinse the seeds well and transfer them to a saucepan. Fill with water and 1 tablespoon salt. Bring to a boil over high heat and continue boiling for 10 minutes. Drain water and pat dry the seeds with a paper towel. Transfer the seeds to a bowl and toss them with the peanut oil and ¼ teaspoon salt. Spread out onto the prepared tray and bake for 20 minutes. Let cool completely on tray before serving.

chocolate peanut butter pie

makes one 9-inch pie

1 Graham Crust (see
page 162)

Mousse

1 (8-ounce) package cream
cheese, at room temperature

2 tablespoons unsalted butter,
at room temperature

1 cup smooth peanut butter

1 cup sugar

1 cup heavy cream, chilled

1 tablespoon pure vanilla
extract

Topping

2 ounces dark chocolate,
chopped

1 tablespoon unsalted butter

1 tablespoon canola oil

½ cup roasted, salted peanuts

Caramel Sauce

¾ cup sugar

¼ cup water

⅛ teaspoon lemon juice

½ cup heavy cream

⅛ teaspoon salt

This pie is meant to revive the memory of your most delicious chocolate and peanut butter experience or to create that memory right here and now. Most of us have seen the ads where two strangers collide, one holding a chocolate bar and the other clinging to a jar of peanut butter. Initial anger is quickly replaced by rapturous joy as they taste the amazing combination. This pie creates that same delicious collision right in your kitchen. Prepare for the happy to happen.

1 Make and bake one 9-inch Graham Crust. Set aside.

2 *Make mousse:* In a mixer with a paddle attachment, beat the cream cheese and butter until smooth and no lumps remain. Scrap bowl well. Beat in peanut butter and sugar until fluffy, about 1 minute. Transfer to a clean bowl.

In a mixer fitted with the whip attachment, mix the heavy cream and vanilla to medium peak. Add one-third of the peanut butter base to the mixer, and whip on low speed until incorporated. Add half of the remaining peanut butter base to the mixer, and whip on low speed until incorporated. Add the remaining base to the cream and whip until incorporated. Increase to medium speed and mix for 1 minute to incorporate air. Transfer mousse to the cooled pie crust. Using a mini offset spatula, spread out the mousse, forming a domed shape, and chill at least 4 hours.

3 *Make topping:* Melt the chocolate, butter, and oil in the microwave, stirring frequently to prevent burning. Pour the chocolate over the mousse and spread as thinly and as quickly as possible using a mini offset spatula. Immediately sprinkle the peanuts over the chocolate. Return to refrigerator to set up for at least 15 minutes before drizzling caramel over the peanuts.

4 Stir together the sugar, water, and lemon juice in a heavy-bottomed small saucepan. Heat the sugar over medium heat until the sugar is dissolved. If necessary, brush the insides of the pan with a wet pastry brush to wash down any crystals sticking to the sides. Increase to high heat and bring to a boil, without stirring, until the sugar reaches a deep amber color, about 4 to 6 minutes.

Remove from heat and carefully whisk in the heavy cream. Be careful as the caramel will sputter as the cream is added. If necessary, return to low heat to melt any clumps of caramel. Stir in the salt. Transfer the caramel to a dish, place in the refrigerator and let cool uncovered.

lemon ricotta cracked cheesecake

Makes one 9-inch cheesecake

I've never understood the paranoia over cracked cheesecakes. In fact, I grew up seeing so many disfigured cheesecakes that I thought they were *supposed* to have cracks in them. Well, my friends, I'm proud to share with all of you my recipe for lemon ricotta cheesecake that will meet your cracked expectations. This cheesecake has the perfect punch of lemon and a moderately dense texture. Yes, one could bake this cheesecake to be crack-less, but what fun is that? A waterbath for three hours? Who has time for that? I'd much rather be at the beach.

1 Preheat oven to 325 degrees. Grease a 9-inch springform pan with pan spray.

2 *Make the crust:* Combine the graham crumbs and sugar in a medium bowl. Mix in the melted butter with your hands. Press the mixture firmly onto the bottom of the pan.

3 *Make the cheesecake batter:* In a mixer fitted with the paddle attachment, beat the cream cheese until smooth. Warm the ricotta in the microwave for 30 seconds. Add to the cream cheese and mix on low speed until smooth, about 2 minutes. Slowly beat in the sugar.

Scrape the bowl. On low speed, add the eggs, heavy cream, and vanilla until batter is smooth. Don't be tempted to increase mixer speed, as you want to minimize the amount of air incorporated into the batter. Scrape the bowl. Fold the lemon zest and juice into the batter.

4 Pour batter over crust. Bake cheesecake 1 hour and 5 minutes. Remove cheesecake from oven and let cool on counter. Refrigerate cheesecake uncovered overnight.

Crust

1½ cups graham cracker crumbs

⅓ cup sugar

¼ cup (½ stick) unsalted butter, melted

Cheesecake batter

2 (8-ounce) packages cream cheese, softened

1 (15-ounce) container ricotta cheese

1⅓ cup sugar

4 large eggs, at room temperature

⅓ cup heavy cream, warm

¼ teaspoons pure vanilla extract

2 teaspoons finely grated lemon zest

¼ cup lemon juice

I recommend using Polly-O Original New York Ricotta. It is much less grainy than others I've tried.

classics

Certain desserts can evoke wonderful memories. For me, these desserts were the ones that I remember having as a child during the hot summer months. So many sweet classics come to mind. I remember always looking forward to having guests visit my parents' home because my mom would make the most amazing berry trifle for them. It's a dessert that I now like to make for my guests. One of my favorite summer classics is my mom's Ruby Cake. I always enjoyed having this pineapple coconut cake, which was passed down to her from her mom. I even remember having poached apricots, definitely not a classic on most people's lists, but I found it a delicious and refreshing change from the typical summer desserts. Really, this chapter is a collection of nostalgic desserts that bring back a smile not only because they were delicious, but also because they take me back to a time when I wasn't calorie counting and life was carefree without the burden of all my responsibilities.

mini tiramisu icebox cakes

Makes 6 (6-ounce) servings

Espresso Syrup
½ cup hot water

2 teaspoons instant espresso

2 teaspoons sugar

Pudding
2 cups whole milk

4 tablespoons cornstarch

2 large egg yolks

½ cup sugar

¼ cup unsweetened cocoa powder

1 cup heavy cream, chilled

Cookie
42 Nabisco Nilla Wafers

This book would be incomplete without an icebox recipe. Icebox cakes became a popular American summer dessert in the 1920s and '30s for their use of pre-made ingredients and quick assembly. My take on this summer dessert is a twist on the classic Italian dessert Tiramisu. I like to serve this dessert in small glass ramekins to show off the layers. Be sure to make this dessert well in advance so it has plenty of time to set up nicely.

1 *Make the syrup:* Mix together water, espresso, and sugar in a small bowl. Set aside.

2 *Make the pudding:* Whisk together 1 cup of the milk, cornstarch, and egg yolks in a small stainless steel bowl. Set aside.

Combine the remaining cup of milk, sugar, and cocoa powder in a medium saucepan. Warm the mixture over medium heat. Whisk the cornstarch mixture into the chocolate mixture and bring the pudding to a boil, stirring continuously. Lower the heat and boil for 1 minute. Pour the pudding into a small bowl and place over a larger bowl filled with ice water. Stir pudding with a rubber spatula until pudding is thick and cool to the touch.

In a mixer fitted with the whip attachment, whip the heavy cream on high speed to medium-stiff peaks. Fold the cream into the pudding with a whisk.

3 *Fill the ramekins:* Place 3 wafers in each ramekin. Sprinkle 1 teaspoon espresso syrup over the wafers. Top the wafers with a dollop of pudding, enough to cover the tops of the wafers. Place 3 more wafers on top of pudding. Sprinkle 1 teaspoon espresso syrup over the wafers. Top with pudding all the way to the rim. Smooth the top. Tap the ramekins on the counter a few times to displace any air bubbles. Place a decorative wafer on top of each ramekin. Place in the refrigerator and let set up at least 3 hours before serving.

berry trifle

Makes one 2-quart trifle

I love making this dessert for summertime barbeques. The presentation is so impressive that many guests don't want to be the first to dig in. I like to use Diplomat cream between the layers, as it is light and fluffy while still having the wonderful creaminess and flavor of pastry cream. I suggest making the components the day before and then assembling the dessert on the day of the get-together.

Day Before

1 *Make simple syrup:* Bring water and sugar to boil over high heat in a small saucepan. Boil for 2 minutes then remove from heat. Store in the refrigerator overnight.

2 *Make angel cake:* Preheat oven to 350 degrees. Line a 9x13x3-inch loaf pan with parchment paper.

Sift together the powdered sugar and flour. Repeat two more times and set aside.

In a mixer fitted with the whip attachment, beat egg whites and cream of tartar on medium speed until foamy. Beat in sugar, 2 tablespoons at a time, on high speed, adding vanilla and salt with the last addition of sugar. Continue beating until stiff and glossy meringue forms. Do not underbeat.

Fold the flour mixture in with a whisk until just incorporated. Gently transfer batter to prepared loaf pan.

3 Bake for 30 to 35 minutes, or until top springs back when pressed gently. Invert pan onto a wire rack for 1 hour. Remove from pan and let cool completely at room temperature.

4 *Make diplomat cream:* Combine the cornstarch, eggs, and ¼ cup of sugar in a medium bowl. Whisk together well.

Place milk and remaining sugar in a saucepan and bring to a boil over high heat. Slowly add the hot milk into the cornstarch mixture while whisking constantly.

Pour the mixture back into the pot. Bring to a boil over medium heat while whisking constantly. Once the mixture has fully thickened, continue cooking and whisking for an additional minute to cook out the starch.

Remove from heat and stir in the butter and vanilla. Pour into a medium bowl, press plastic wrap onto the surface of the pudding, and place in the refrigerator overnight.

Day Of

5 *Finish diplomat cream:* In a mixer fitted with the whip attachment, mix the heavy cream and sugar to medium-stiff peaks on high speed. Fold one-third of the cream into the pastry cream using a whisk. Repeat step until all the cream is incorporated.

6 *Assemble trifle:* Pick 3 large pretty strawberries and set aside. Hull and slice the remaining strawberries and place in a medium bowl. Toss them with the raspberry jam.

7 Cut the angel cake in ½-inch cubes. Use one-third of the cake cubes to line the bottom of the trifle bowl. Using a spoon, sprinkle some simple syrup over the cake cubes. Spoon (or pipe) some diplomat cream over the cake. Layer the blueberries over the cream. Arrange another third of the cake cubes over the blueberries. Sprinkle some simple syrup over the cake cubes. Spoon (or pipe) some diplomat cream over the cake. Arrange the raspberries along the outside rim of the cream. Fill the center with some strawberries. Arrange the last third of the cake cubes over the raspberries. Sprinkle the remaining simple syrup over the cake cubes. Spoon (or pipe) the remaining diplomat cream over the cake. Arrange blackberries along the outside rim of the cream. Fill the center with the remaining strawberries. Place the 3 whole strawberries in the very center. Keep chilled until serving time.

Simple Syrup

1 cup water

⅓ cup sugar

Angel Cake

¾ cup powdered sugar

½ cup cake flour

6 large egg whites, at room temperature

¾ teaspoon cream of tartar

½ cup sugar

1 teaspoon pure vanilla extract

⅛ teaspoon salt

Diplomat cream

¼ cup cornstarch

2 large eggs

½ cup sugar

2 cups whole milk

1 tablespoon unsalted butter, at room temperature

1 teaspoon pure vanilla extract

1½ cups heavy cream, chilled

3 tablespoons sugar

Berries

1 (16-ounce) package strawberries

1 tablespoon raspberry jam

1 (4.4-ounce) package blueberries

1 (6-ounce) package raspberries

1 (6-ounce) package blackberries

ruby cake ★

Cake

2 large eggs

1½ cups sugar

⅓ cup vegetable oil

1 (20-ounce) can crushed pineapple

2 cups all-purpose flour, sifted

2 teaspoons baking soda

½ teaspoon salt

1 cup sweetened coconut flakes

1 cup walnuts, chopped

Icing

½ cup (1 stick) unsalted butter, at room temperature

½ cup sugar

1 (5-ounce) can evaporated milk

1 teaspoon pure vanilla extract

This recipe was passed down to my mom from her mom, and it has been a staple in our household ever since I can remember. As soon as this pineapple coconut cake is removed from the oven, it is soaked with a warm butter icing that seeps down into the cake, keeping it moist for days. I hope you enjoy it as much as I do.

1 Preheat the oven to 350 degrees. Grease a 9x13-inch baking dish with pan spray.

2 *Make the cake:* In a large bowl, mix the eggs, sugar, and oil with a wooden spoon. Stir in the crushed pineapple. Add the flour, baking soda, and salt, and mix until incorporated. Do not overmix. Pour the batter into the prepared cake pan. Sprinkle the coconut on top and bake for 38 to 40 minutes or until an inserted toothpick comes out clean. Sprinkle the walnuts over the cake. Set aside and make the icing.

3 *Make the icing:* Bring all the ingredients to a boil and cook till the sugar melts. Pour the hot icing over the warm cake. Let soak for 10 minutes before serving.

Make sure to make this cake by hand. Using an electric mixer will result in a dense cake.

baked apple cider donuts ★⏰

Makes about 8 donuts

1 cup all-purpose flour

⅓ cup sugar

½ teaspoon baking powder

½ teaspoon baking soda

½ teaspoon ground cinnamon

¼ teaspoon ground nutmeg

1 large egg

¼ cup apple cider

¼ cup buttermilk

¼ cup canola oil

½ teaspoon pure vanilla extract

Sugar for coating

Every fall, my family and I would visit our favorite apple orchard in New Jersey. I remember as a child peering into their bakery cases packed with rows of sugar-coated apple cider donuts. We would buy a bag full of donuts, take them home, and savor each one. After moving out West, I didn't make it back there as often as I wanted to and my annual apple cider donut cravings went unfulfilled. After numerous failed attempts to get them to share their recipe with me, I resigned myself to the fact that I would have to develop my own version to satisfy my craving every time apple season rolled around. Well, I'm over the moon excited about the outcome. These donuts are light, fluffy, and sugary with a hint of autumn. These donuts stay soft for days if you can resist them that long!

1 Preheat the oven to 350 degrees. Grease a Wilton 6-cavity donut pan with pan spray.

2 In a large bowl, whisk together the flour, sugar, baking powder, baking soda, cinnamon, and nutmeg. In a separate bowl, whisk together the egg, cider, buttermilk, oil, and vanilla. Pour the wet ingredients onto the dry ingredients and mix together thoroughly.

3 Using a pastry bag fitted with the ½-inch smooth round tip, pipe the batter into the donut molds just over half way. Bake 5 minutes. Rotate the pan and then bake for an additional 5 minutes or until the donut tops spring back slightly when pressed. Remove from oven and let cool in the pan for 10 minutes before inverting the donuts onto a wire rack.

4 Fill a medium bowl with sugar. Toss the donuts in the sugar.

If the sugar coating melts from the humidity, simply re-coat the donuts right before serving.

caramel apple skillet cake

Makes one 12-inch cast iron skillet cake

When the cooler weather hits the coast, I always pull out this cake recipe. Don't be turned off by the thought of making caramel, as it is completely worth the effort and not as difficult as you may expect. The apples are tossed in vanilla, cinnamon, and cardamom and then cooked in the caramel, allowing the apples to infuse the spiced caramel essence.

1 Preheat oven to 375 degrees.

2 *Caramelize the apples:* Peel, core, and slice apples in ¼-inch thick wedges and place in a large bowl. Add the butter, vanilla, cinnamon, and cardamom. Toss to coat and set aside.

In a very clean medium sauté pan, combine the sugar, water, and the lemon juice over medium heat. Boil until the mixture turns golden amber. Remove from heat and slowly add the apples. Be careful, as some caramel may splash up. Return to low heat. Carefully stir the apples with a rubber spatula until butter is melted and the apples are coated with caramel. Continue cooking at a low boil, stirring occasionally until apples are tender, about 8 minutes. Remove from heat.

3 *Make the cake:* In a mixer fitted with the paddle attachment, mix the egg, buttermilk, and vanilla on medium speed until combined. Add the flour, sugar, baking powder, and salt and mix on low speed until smooth.

Warm the skillet on stovetop over medium heat. Add butter. Coat the bottom of the pan with the sizzling butter. Turn off heat and pour in cake batter. Using tongs, strain the apples from the caramel (save the caramel for later) and arrange the fruit evenly on top of the batter. Immediately place skillet in oven.

4 Bake for 15 minutes. Remove from oven and let sit for 5 minutes. Cake may look underdone but will continue baking in the hot skillet. Serve warm over a puddle of the reserved caramel and a sprinkling of powdered sugar.

Caramel apples

1½ pounds Fuji apples

2 tablespoons unsalted butter, at room temperature

1 teaspoon pure vanilla extract

½ teaspoon ground cinnamon

¼ teaspoon ground cardamon

¾ cup sugar

¼ cup water

½ teaspoon lemon juice

Cake

1 large egg

½ cup buttermilk

1 teaspoon pure vanilla extract

1 cup cake flour, sifted

¾ cup sugar

1½ teaspoons baking powder

¼ teaspoon salt

2 tablespoons unsalted butter, at room temperature

Powdered sugar for sprinkling

honey vanilla poached apricots gv

Makes 4 servings

1 cup filtered water

¼ cup clover honey

½ vanilla bean

1 pound fresh ripe California apricots, halved lengthwise and pitted (about 4 large apricots)

1 tablespoon Amaretto

Greek-style yogurt, optional (I prefer Fage)

Toward the end of May and early June, California apricots start popping up in grocery stores and farmers' markets. This is a sure sign that summer is approaching. I like to keep it simple and poach my apricots with honey and vanilla bean (not extract). The perfume-like aroma that fills your kitchen as they poach in the syrup is divine. As you take a bite of the warm apricots and cool yogurt, imagine yourself relaxing under swaying palms as the warm Pacific air surrounds you.

1 In a small saucepan, combine filtered water and honey. Split vanilla bean in half lengthwise. Scrape out the seeds and add both seeds and pod to saucepan. Bring to a boil over medium-high heat. Whisk mixture to break up vanilla bean clumps. Add apricots, cover, reduce heat to low and simmer until just tender, about 4 to 5 minutes depending on the ripeness of the fruit.

2 Transfer the poached apricots with a slotted spoon to a dish and discard the vanilla pod. Boil the remaining syrup uncovered until reduced to about ½ cup. Remove from heat and stir in the Amaretto. Serve warm with a generous drizzle of the thickened syrup and a dollop of yogurt if desired. The fruit will keep in an airtight container for 2 days in the refrigerator.

bonus recipes

almond squares ★☼⏰

Makes one 9x13x2-inch pan

I was given a version of this almond bar recipe by a baker I met in Georgia while traveling through the state on my way to the unspoiled beaches of Cumberland Island. To this day, the tranquil environment of Cumberland takes my breath away. Royal bloodline wild horses roam the many acres of undeveloped beaches, maritime forests, and marshes there. It's a sight worth seeing and it remains one of my favorite beach memories.

2 large eggs

¾ cup sugar

1 teaspoon pure vanilla extract

½ teaspoon salt

1 cup (2 sticks) unsalted butter, melted

1 cup all-purpose flour

1 Preheat the oven to 350 degrees. Grease a 9x13x2-inch pan with pan spray and set aside.

2 Combine the eggs, sugar, vanilla, and salt in a mixer fitted with the paddle attachment and beat until thick, about 2 minutes. Mix in the butter and flour until incorporated. Pour batter into prepared pan and bake for 25 minutes.

3 Combine all the topping ingredients in a small pot and cook over low heat. Stir constantly until sugar is dissolved and mixture thickens. Spread the mixture over the cake right after it comes out of the oven. Adjust the oven to high broil and caramelize the topping for 6 minutes, rotating the pan every 2 minutes. Cool completely before cutting into squares.

Almond Topping

½ cup (1 stick) unsalted butter

½ cup sugar

½ cup sliced almonds

1 tablespoon all-purpose flour

1 tablespoon whole milk

flourless chocolate torte 9

Makes one 9-inch torte

½ pound dark chocolate, chopped

½ cup (1 stick) unsalted butter, soft

2 tablespoons coffee liquor (I prefer Kahlua)

4 large eggs

1 teaspoon pure vanilla extract

¼ teaspoon salt

Ganache Layer

½ cup heavy cream

¾ cup dark chocolate, chopped

This decadent gluten-free chocolate torte is always a showstopper. Two layers of dark chocolate make the perfect dessert for that special occasion. The top layer of super smooth ganache blends seamlessly with the flourless cake below. Feel free to omit the coffee liquor if you desire—it will still be delicious.

1 Preheat oven to 350 degrees. Grease a 9-inch round cake pan and line the bottom with parchment paper. Set aside.

2 Place the chocolate, butter, and coffee liquor in a double boiler over simmering water and stir until melted. Remove bowl and set aside to cool.

3 Combine the eggs, vanilla, and salt in a mixer fitted with the whip attachment. Beat on high until doubled in volume, about 5 minutes. Gently fold in one-third of the chocolate mixture into the whipped eggs. Repeat this step two more times with the remaining chocolate mixture. Transfer the batter to the prepared pan. Bake for 25 minutes. Remove from oven and let set up in refrigerator overnight. The middle will sink slightly.

4 *The next day:* Run a paring knife around the edges of the torte. Flip out onto a serving plate. Set aside.

5 Add the cream to a small pot and bring to a boil over high heat. Remove from heat and add the chocolate. Let sit for 1 minute. Stir until chocolate is melted and ganache is smooth. Pour onto the torte and use a mini offset spatula to evenly spread the ganache. Place in refrigerator for at least 30 minutes before serving.

banana date shake g🕐v♥

Makes two servings

This is the perfect morning treat when you're short on time and rushing out to the beach or to work. If you're like me, your freezer is packed with overripe bananas, and this vegan shake is a great way to start putting them toward a tasty use!

○○

1 Place all ingredients in a blender and purée until smooth, about 1 minute. Serve immediately.

2 large frozen bananas, slightly thawed

1 cup vanilla almond milk, cold

⅓ cup deglet noor dates, chopped

½ teaspoon ground cinnamon

sunny peach pie
Makes one 9-inch pie

2 Sweet Butter Crusts (see page 160)

3½ pounds yellow peaches

1 cup sugar

⅓ cup all-purpose flour

1 tablespoon lemon juice

½ teaspoon ground cinnamon

¼ teaspoon salt

1 large egg white, whisked

2 tablespoons turbinado sugar

Filled with juicy peaches and topped with a sugary crust, this peach pie shines like the sun. The filling is packed with a boat-load of fresh yellow peaches and is flavored with cinnamon and a generous dose of sugar.

1 Preheat oven to 450 degrees and place a sheet tray on the bottom rack. This will be used to catch any juices that bubble over.

2 Prepare 2 Sweet Butter Crusts. Roll out half the dough onto a 9-inch pie plate, leaving a ½-inch overhang. Place pie shell in the refrigerator until needed. Roll out the remaining dough into a 12-inch circle and transfer to a large plate or sheet tray. Use a small cutter to cut out decorative shapes in the dough if desired. Place in refrigerator until needed.

3 Peel the peaches, remove the pits, and cut into wedges (I get about 10 wedges per peach). Place the cut fruit into a large bowl and toss well with the sugar, flour, lemon juice, cinnamon, and salt. Remove the pie shell from the refrigerator and fill it with the fruit mixture, forming a mound. Brush the edges of pie dough with the whisked egg white. Lay the second pie crust on top and crimp edges to seal. Brush the top with the egg white and sprinkle with the turbinado sugar. Bake on the middle rack for 10 minutes. Reduce oven temperature to 350 degrees and bake for 30 minutes more or until the juices bubble over. Let pie rest on counter for at least 30 minutes before serving.

fresh strawberry pie

Makes one 9-inch pie

Memories of picking strawberries with my mom during the warm summer months always flood my mind when I eat this pie. Among the long rows of plants, the aroma of the ripe berries rose off the ground with the heat and it was impossible not to pop one or two into my mouth as we were picking the fruit. Thankfully, the farm owners allowed their customers to sample a few along the way! The gorgeous red filling oozes from every slice of this pie while the crunchy pecan oat streusel complements the soft berries below.

1 Preheat oven to 375 degrees and place a sheet tray on the middle rack. You will bake the pie on this tray.

2 Prepare 1 Sweet Butter Crust. Roll out the dough onto a 9-inch pie plate, leaving a ½-inch overhang. Fold overhang under to be flush with edge of pie plate and flute as desired. Poke holes in the dough with a fork, line the shell with a piece of parchment paper, and fill with baking beans or rice. Bake for 10 minutes. Remove from oven and let cool on counter. Reduce oven temperature to 350 degrees.

3 Place the strawberries in a large bowl. Measure out 1½ cups of the berries and transfer them to a medium pot. Add the sugar, corn starch, and vanilla to the pot and cook over medium heat. Cook at a low boil for 2 minutes until thickened, stirring constantly, and mashing the strawberries as they cook. Transfer the paste to the large bowl and stir into the remaining strawberries. Set aside.

4 Combine the flour, oats, brown sugar, cinnamon, and salt in a mixer fitted with the paddle attachment. Add the cubed butter and mix on low speed until butter breaks down to pea size. Mix in the pecans on low speed just until combined.

5 Fill the par-baked pie shell with the strawberry filling. Top with the pecan streusel. Bake for 25 minutes or until filling bubbles and topping is golden brown. Let pie rest on counter for at least 30 minutes before serving.

1 Sweet Butter Crust (see page 160)

Strawberry Filling

2 pounds strawberries, hulled and quartered

⅓ cup sugar

¼ cup corn starch

1 teaspoon pure vanilla extract

Pecan Streusel

⅓ cup all-purpose flour

⅓ cup rolled oats

⅓ cup brown sugar

½ teaspoon ground cinnamon

¼ teaspoon salt

4 tablespoons unsalted butter, cold and cubed

⅓ cup chopped pecans

mint julep

Makes 2 servings

2 tablespoons sugar

8 spearmint leaves, torn

4 ounces whiskey (I like Woodford Reserve)

4 cups crushed ice

Fresh spearmint sprigs, for garnish

This classic Southern whiskey-based cocktail is packed with spearmint, sweetened with sugar, and chilled with lots of crushed ice. It's a refreshing beverage that wakes up your senses so you can breathe in the salty air of the ocean.

1 Combine the sugar and ¼ cup water in a small pot and warm over medium heat until sugar dissolves. Remove from heat and stir in the torn mint leaves. Steep for 5 minutes.

2 Combine the whiskey, crushed ice, and the mint simple syrup in a tall glass and stir to combine. Pour into two drinking glasses and garnish with fresh spearmint.

popovers

Makes 8 popovers

These light and airy pastries make delightful breakfast treats. On cool breezy mornings by the beach, I love to enjoy warm, just-baked popovers slathered with fresh strawberry butter. Their moist, tender interior is a lovely contrast to their browned crispy exterior. Hollow in the center and light as clouds—plan on eating more than just one.

3 large eggs

2 tablespoons canola oil

1 cup whole milk

1 teaspoon sugar

½ teaspoon salt

1 cup all-purpose flour

1 Preheat the oven to 425 degrees. Place a sheet tray on the top rack. Remove the middle rack and place a 12-cup muffin pan on the lower rack.

2 When oven is ready, add all the ingredients to a blender in the order listed. Mix on high speed for 30 seconds until ingredients are incorporated. Remove the muffin pan from the oven and grease the entire top of the pan well with pan spray. Fill each muffin cup two-thirds full with the batter. Bake on the lower rack for 15 minutes. Reduce oven temperature to 350 degrees and bake for 25 minutes more. Do not open the oven door during the entire baking period. Remove popovers from oven and serve immediately.

lemon poppyseed loaf ☀

Makes one 9x5x3-inch loaf

Loaf

2 large eggs

1 cup sugar

¾ cup buttermilk

⅓ cup unsalted butter, melted

¼ cup lemon juice

1 tablespoon lemon zest

½ teaspoon pure lemon extract

½ teaspoon pure vanilla extract

2½ cups cake flour, sifted

1 tablespoon baking powder

1 tablespoon poppy seeds

½ teaspoon salt

Glaze

1 cup powdered sugar, sifted

2 tablespoons unsalted butter, soft

2 tablespoons lemon juice

This is a moist, sweet-tart quick bread that is delicious any time of day. The warm loaf is topped with a sweet lemon glaze that adds an additional pop of lemon flavor. The bread's buttery crumb, soft texture, and poppy seed crunch make it delightfully delicious.

1 Preheat oven to 325 degrees. Grease a 9x5x3-inch loaf pan and set aside.

2 In a mixer fitted with the paddle attachment, beat the eggs, sugar, buttermilk, butter, lemon juice, zest, and extracts until incorporated. Add the flour, baking powder, poppy seeds, and salt and mix on low speed until incorporated. Scrape bowl well. Transfer batter to prepared loaf pan and bake for 1 hour or until an inserted toothpick comes out clean. Remove from oven and let cool on counter while you prepare glaze.

3 In a mixer fitted with the paddle attachment, beat all the ingredients on low speed until smooth. Scrape bowl well. Run a paring knife carefully around the edges of the loaf and invert onto a cooling rack. Pour the glaze over the warm loaf. Let cool completely before slicing.

margarita cupcakes

Makes 12 cupcakes

With one bite of this lime and tequila cupcake, you will be whisked away to the stunning beaches of Playa del Carmen, a coastal resort town on the Yucatán Peninsula of Mexico. I loved vacationing there, alternating tranquil days on the beach with active outings exploring the Mayan ruins of Tulum.

1 Preheat the oven to 325 degrees. Line cupcake pan with 12 paper liners.

2 Sift the cake flour, baking powder, and salt. Set aside.

3 In a mixer fitted with the paddle attachment, cream the butter, sugar, lime zest, and vanilla on medium speed until light and fluffy, about 2 minutes. Mix in the eggs one at a time, scraping well after each addition. With the mixer on low speed, add the milk and dry ingredients alternately, beginning with the milk and ending with the flour. Mix in the tequila and lime juice. Scrape bowl well.

4 Scoop the batter into the cupcake liners, filling them just below the rim. (I use a 2-ounce ice cream scoop.) Bake in the center of the oven for 22 to 24 minutes or until a toothpick comes out clean. Cool for 10 minutes, remove from the pan, and allow to cool completely before frosting.

5 *Make the frosting:* Sift the powdered sugar and set aside.

6 In a mixer fitted with the paddle attachment, cream the butter on medium speed until very smooth and soft. Add the sifted powdered sugar to the butter and mix on low speed until incorporated. Add the lime juice, tequila, and vanilla. Mix on medium speed for 2 minutes to ensure that the frosting is light and fluffy.

1¼ cups cake flour

1 teaspoon baking powder

½ teaspoon salt

½ cup (1 stick) unsalted butter, at room temperature

1 cup sugar

Zest of one lime

½ teaspoon pure vanilla extract

2 large eggs

½ cup whole milk

2 tablespoons tequila (I prefer Hornitos Reposado)

2 tablespoons fresh lime juice

Frosting

2½ cups powdered sugar

1 cup (2 sticks) unsalted butter, at room temperature

1 tablespoon fresh lime juice

1 tablespoon tequila

½ teaspoon pure vanilla extract

strawberry daiquiri cupcakes

Makes 14 cupcakes

Roasted Strawberries

12 ounces strawberries, hulled and halved

1 teaspoon sugar

Cupcakes

1 cup cake flour

2 teaspoons baking powder

¼ teaspoon salt

3 ounces unsalted butter, at room temperature

1 cup sugar

Zest of one lime

1 teaspoon pure vanilla extract

2 large eggs

¼ cup evaporated milk

2 tablespoons rum (I prefer Bacardi)

Frosting

2 cups heavy cream, chilled

½ cup powdered sugar, sifted

1 teaspoon pure vanilla extract

A strawberry daiquiri was the first cocktail I ever tried. I was vacationing in Saint Thomas spending my days laying on the beach and snorkeling the clear blue waters of the US Virgin Islands. Just like its cocktail version, these strawberry daiquiri cupcakes combine strawberries, sugar, lime, and rum to make a sweet treat that can be enjoyed any time of day. Roasting the strawberries ahead of time intensifies not only their sweet flavor but also their beautiful red color, eliminating the need for any artificial coloring or additives.

1 Preheat the oven to 350 degrees. Line two cupcake pans with 14 paper liners and set aside.

2 Combine the strawberries and 1 teaspoon sugar in a large bowl. Transfer to a 9-inch pie plate and roast in the oven for 45 minutes, stirring once halfway. Remove from oven and let cool for 10 minutes. Purée in a blender until smooth. Set aside.

3 Sift the cake flour, baking powder, and salt. Set aside.

4 In a mixer fitted with the paddle attachment, cream the butter, sugar, lime zest, and vanilla on medium speed until light and fluffy, about 2 minutes. Mix in the eggs one at a time, scraping well after each addition. With the mixer on low speed, add the milk and dry ingredients alternately, beginning with the milk and ending with the flour. Mix in the rum and the strawberry purée. Scrape bowl well.

5 Scoop the batter into the cupcake liners, filling them up to the rim. (I use a 2.6-ounce ice cream scoop.) Bake in the center of the oven for 20 to 22 minutes or until a toothpick comes out clean. Cool for 10 minutes, remove from the pan, and allow to cool completely before frosting.

6 *Make the frosting:* Combine all ingredients in a mixer fitted with the whip attachment. Beat on low speed until the mixture begins to thicken. Increase speed to medium and continue mixing until cream is stiff yet smooth. Transfer to a piping bag and frost the cooled cupcakes.

acknowledgments

My literary agent Deborah Ritchken for believing in this book from the start when others had doubts.

My editor Nicole Frail for your sage advice and assistance in polishing my manuscript. I have truly enjoyed working on this book with you.

The Skyhorse Publishing team for making one of my dreams come true.

My photographer Chau Vuong for making my baked creations look spectacular. I am so glad we met, and I truly hope we work on another book together.

My employees at Sugar Blossom for assisting with recipe testing and managing the bakery so I could focus on writing.

My parents, brother, and friends for enthusiastically supporting me along the way.

My dear friend Tammy for your help with the Introduction and always being so proud of me.

My PK for always making me smile.

My G, I could not have written this book without you.

index

Ruby Beach, Washington, 182
ruby cake, 193, 198–*199*
rum, 60, 67

S

salt, xviii, 70
San Clemente, *4–5*
San Onofre State Park, 42
sangria, *26–27*
santorini exalted, *108–109*
scale, xiv
scones, *2–3*, *16–17*
Shirahama Beach, Japan, 94
sieves/sifters, xv
Silver Beach, Beihai City (China), 143
simple syrup, 197
SKOR toffee bits, 94, 119
s'mores cupcakes, *42–43*
snickerdoodle, *78–79*
South Florida, 77
spatulas, xv
spring form pan, xiv
Sri Lanka, 156
st. barths, *128–129*
stainless steel bowls, xiv
strawberries, 27, 144, 151, 175, 185, 197
strawberry daiquiri cupcakes, *226–227*
strawberry frozen pop, *150*–151
strawberry rhubarb honey crisp, *184–185*
sugar, xvii
Sugar Blossom, x, xiii, 37, 46, 63, 78, 121
sugar layouts, *98–99*
sunbursts, *120–121*
sunny peach pie, *214–215*
surfer cowboy coffee, *32–33*
surfin p.b.j., *50–51*
sweet and salty beach bod brittle, *84–85*
sweet butter crust, 160
symbol guide for recipes, xix

T

tangerines, 148

tarragon, 144
tea, 24–*25*, 34–*35*, 143, 156
the best hot cocoa, *30–31*
the ultimate road trip cookie, *100–101*
thermometer, xiii, xv
tiramisu, 194–*195*
Tofino, B.C., 16
tools, xiii–xvi
torch, xvi
Torrey Pines State Reserve, 132
trays (baking/sheet), xiv
trifle, *196–197*
tropical carrot cupcakes with ginger frosting, *52–53*
Tropical Islands Resort (Krausnick, Germany), 45
tropical tea, *24–25*
tsunamis, *94–95*
Tulum, Mexico, 93

V

vanilla extract, 38
Virginia Beach, 82

W

waffle press, xiv
wafflecakes, *6–7*
waimea bay, *126–127*
walnuts, 108, 119, 136, 198
watermelon frozen pop, 140–*141*
whiskey glaze, 96
Whitehaven Beach, Australia, 181
whoopee pies, *106–107*
windswept cherry pie, *182–183*
wine, 64

Y

yogurt, 155

cookbook conversions charts

METRIC AND IMPERIAL CONVERSIONS

(These conversions are rounded for convenience)

Ingredient	Cups/Tablespoons/ Teaspoons	Ounces	Grams/Milliliters
Butter	1 cup=16 tablespoons= 2 sticks	8 ounces	230 grams
Cream cheese	1 tablespoon	0.5 ounce	14.5 grams
Cheese, shredded	1 cup	4 ounces	110 grams
Cornstarch	1 tablespoon	0.3 ounce	8 grams
Flour, all-purpose	1 cup/1 tablespoon	4.5 ounces/0.3 ounce	125 grams/8 grams
Flour, whole wheat	1 cup	4 ounces	120 grams
Fruit, dried	1 cup	4 ounces	120 grams
Fruits or veggies, chopped	1 cup	5 to 7 ounces	145 to 200 grams
Fruits or veggies, puréed	1 cup	8.5 ounces	245 grams
Honey, maple syrup, or corn syrup	1 tablespoon	.75 ounce	20 grams
Liquids: cream, milk, water, or juice	1 cup	8 fluid ounces	240 milliliters
Oats	1 cup	5.5 ounces	150 grams
Salt	1 teaspoon	0.2 ounces	6 grams
Spices: cinnamon, cloves, ginger, or nutmeg (ground)	1 teaspoon	0.2 ounce	5 milliliters
Sugar, brown, firmly packed	1 cup	7 ounces	200 grams
Sugar, white	1 cup/1 tablespoon	7 ounces/0.5 ounce	200 grams/12.5 grams
Vanilla extract	1 teaspoon	0.2 ounce	4 grams

OVEN TEMPERATURES

Fahrenheit	Celcius	Gas Mark
225°	110°	¼
250°	120°	½
275°	140°	1
300°	150°	2
325°	160°	3
350°	180°	4
375°	190°	5
400°	200°	6
425°	220°	7
450°	230°	8